M000188004

BYPASSED

Copyright © 2020 Alec Hanson

All rights reserved. No part of this publication may be reproduced, distributed, or transmitted in any form or by any means, including photocopying, recording, or other electronic or mechanical methods, without the prior written permission of the publisher, except in the case of brief quotations embodied in critical reviews and certain other non-commercial uses permitted by copyright law. For permission requests, write to the publisher, addressed "Attention: Permissions Coordinator," at the address below.

 Modern Spartan
PO Box 10994
Costa Mesa, CA 92627

ISBN: 978-1-7345783-0-0 (print)
ISBN: 978-1-7345783-1-7 (ebook)

Ordering Information:

Special discounts are available on quantity purchases by corporations, associations, and others. For details, contact Alec at 949-500-8062

BYPASSED

A MODERN GUIDE *for* LOCAL MORTGAGE PROS
LEFT BEHIND BY THE DIGITAL CUSTOMER

ALEC HANSON

CONTENTS

Dedication

This book is dedicated to the men and women who decided to turn the camera around and share their stories and to the men and women who serve our great country and protect and defend our freedoms every day. I chose the first group because they step into discomfort to change *their* lives and the second group because they step into danger so we can change *ours*.

I'd also like to thank my beautiful wife Erica, who somehow finds a way to love a driven, competitive, sometimes annoying and nerdy introvert. Love you, babe!

And to my wonderful mom, dad, and sister (Dan, Durene, and Kristin). I'm who I am today because of the foundation of love (even the tough kind), support, and encouragement you give me even to this day!

PROLOGUE

Working in the mortgage industry can often be compared to riding a roller coaster blindfolded. Sometimes you think you know where you are going only to experience a dramatic turn, a sharp drop, or a full on loop the loop. I began my personal journey to re-arm and re-train the local mortgage professional back in 2018, never knowing it would turn into an amazing training program known as the Modern Lending Playbook for loanDepot. Now, on the cusp of publishing this book, I find myself once again on the roller coaster ride of a lifetime.

Back in 2018, the mortgage industry was shrinking. Rates were moving upward, margin compression was very real, and the industry was about to go through a major consolidation even though the general economy was doing very well. Fast forward to 2020 and we find ourselves in the midst of a major industry and national economic crisis. The coronavirus pandemic is sweeping the globe. The major markets in the United States and all around the world are trying to navigate this unprecedented market chaos and the mortgage industry, well, let's just say the comparison to a roller-coaster is dead on.

Interest rates plummeted. Mortgage companies, on

the cusp of going out of business, suddenly had more loan applications than they could handle. The entire industry ballooned as more and more customers applied for a refinance or a purchase loan than ever before. This, of course, is introducing different and more complex problems for the mortgage industry, both due to the increase in volume and due to the global economic crisis we are all facing.

I felt compelled to address these dramatic events in the prologue of this book as a warning. In 2018, the dominos were starting to line up, forecasting a very real threat to the local mortgage professional's way of originating business. Up to 2020, that threat was increasing, making it even more imperative that local mortgage pros change their mindsets and skill sets in order to remain relevant. This influx of new business, this wave of refinance loans hitting the market right now is only masking this very real and very dangerous threat. With full pipelines and irrational short-sightedness, many mortgage pros will take their eyes off the ball. They will get complacent and lazy. They will start acting like gluttons at an all-you-can-eat buffet, ignoring the fact that closing time is coming. And when it does come and the patrons are shuffled, full and bloated, out into the streets, there will be a price to pay.

Those who heed this warning, those who remain diligent to evolving their businesses and paying the price to learn new skills and master new tools, those amazing local mortgage professionals will inherit this amazing industry, the rest will simply be bypassed.

PART I

BUILDING YOUR DIGITAL BRAND

CHAPTER 1

Don't Worry, You Won't Become Famous

I f homebuyers want to look for a home today, where would they start?

The answer to this question is very different today than it was 15 years ago. In the past, homebuyers had to turn to a real estate agent. Back then, the general public, including the mortgage professionals, didn't know all of the homes that were for sale in the community. Listing services, like what Zillow and Realtor.com use today, were locked down and exclusive to real estate agents, so mortgage professionals had no idea what was for sale unless they drove around town, looked for yard signs, or checked a newspaper to see what open houses were happening that weekend. The way they got customers in the mortgage business was to prospect, partner, and solicit real estate agents and try to develop a relationship. So when that customer went to that real estate agent to find that house, that real estate agent referred them to a mortgage professional to do their loans.

Fast forward 15 years, and now the potential home-buyer doesn't need to go to a local real estate agent first. They can go online and get tons of information, often a lot of misinformation, about homes that are for sale and the mortgage process. Currently, the number one lender in the country is internet-based (their ads usually run during the Super Bowl). The reason that company is the leading lender in the country right now is because it exists where potential homebuyers are searching for information on homes and mortgages. What's interesting about internet-based companies is that their mortgage professionals are likely to have fewer than five years of experience in the business. That's not a knock on those young professionals; it's just reality.

Here's the scary thing about the world moving toward this internet-first type of experience: The professional mortgage experts, many with 30 years of experience, who live in their local communities, have become virtually invisible to the local homebuyers. Those veteran salespeople seem to have lost their relevance. Many are sitting around asking, "Where did my business go?" The local real estate agents they partnered with are losing their ability to refer people because the customer is starting to drive the real estate transaction. In the past, a real estate professional drove 99 percent of the transaction by referring, controlling, and encouraging the customers down their path with their preferred lender and title and escrow company, along with ancillary services. These veteran mortgage professionals who are slowly becoming invisible work for 100-percent commission, so if they don't close a loan, they can't feed their families. And that puts them under a lot of pressure.

We're at a crossroads today. I work with salespeople who started out doing 10 loans a month and then that went down to five. Some of them are down to two, and it's not because they aren't good at what they do. Some of them are total badasses! They're talented, authentic, and they care about the customer. They have done thousands of loans across the country, and many are true doctors of their craft, but fewer and fewer people are working with them anymore. It doesn't help that a stigma continues to surround mortgage professionals that puts them one rung above used-car salesmen. That is a tragedy given the knowledge and support these professionals have provided customers over the years.

Today, the loan industry has an aging salesforce whose skill set in finding customers is nearly obsolete. The industry is passing them by and is beginning to squeeze them out. Thinking back to the American credit crisis in 2008, it was a massive change that forced mortgage professionals to adjust how they did business. Mortgage companies began imploding and going out of business. Loan products that had been available simply ceased to exist. What a loan consultant did to find and earn business no longer worked and many left the industry entirely. Those who decided to stay had to change to stay relevant.

What the mortgage industry is going through now is almost on the same level as that crisis, but the change is occurring at a much slower rate. These current changes in consumer behavior are causing some mortgage professionals to slowly become irrelevant. They don't realize their businesses and their strategies are under pressure to change. Many are putting their heads in the sand and clinging to the old way of business.

The great news is that not all is lost. There is a path forward for those salespeople, and I'm passionate about showing it to them. This book is a rallying cry to get them to wake up and understand, not just that the world has changed, but how they need to adapt and what skill sets they need to develop to survive and thrive as mortgage professionals in the world today. This is a blueprint for how to make the invisible mortgage professional visible once again.

I started in this business in 2004. I drove around to open houses with printouts from MapQuest and my rock-solid Nokia cell phone with the goal of meeting local real estate agents, establishing trust and relationships, and earning their referral business. I know exactly what it takes and I have earned my stripes. I was Rookie of the Year that year, recognized across the country in what is now called the Scotsman Guide, funding $85,000,000 that year. My personal best was close to $200,000,000 a few years later. I originated in the environment described above. I managed a dynamic team of rock stars through the credit crisis and saw firsthand the carnage it caused.

But I was also raised a digital native. I'm a millennial. I was raised on the Oregon Trail, and had a cell phone in my hand the day they became mainstream. I was online with AOL when it was chat rooms, surfed on Napster, grew up in Facebook, and even had a profile on Friendster, Myspace, etc. Because of that background, as well as seeing what is happening to my industry, I know what needs to be done.

How Visible Is Your Brand?

Let's not get hung up on "brand" as a buzzword. Instead, let's look at what it really means. A brand is not your tagline or some ugly personal logo you may have tried to create on your computer. In this context, your brand is your digital reputation. If you're old school like me, the words "reputation" and "character" mean something very similar.

When someone Googles your name, what will they find? How do you come across to the general public? Like it or not, the result of that search is a vivid indication of what you have to offer. It will convey your past performance and potential value to customers. In some ways, it could be considered a promise.

Think about when you're referred to a professional in any industry. You will probably look them up. You'll research their company, read reviews, and pull up their digital brand. Let's say you're given two names. The first person is a 20-year veteran and a total badass but nothing comes up during an online search. The second person might be 30 years old and have only five years of experience but he's got 300 five-star reviews on Yelp, a video series on YouTube, and a great web page. You poke around his social media pages, and suddenly it feels like you've built rapport with that person. You're more comfortable with the second person, so who are you going to call?

It's important to remember that not everyone starts on an equal playing field when it comes to building a brand and an online presence. This is a skill that comes naturally to some, and they will have a leg up on those who struggle to navigate through a foreign social media landscape. That's okay. It's not the end of the world. That's why you're here. Building a brand is something everyone can do, but it won't always be easy. There will be some growing pains, and you will be forced to get out of your comfort zone. But you're in an age where you have to adapt or die, so what choice do you really have?

Before you get started, I can't emphasize enough that you must have patience and trust the process. This is a marathon, not a sprint. This is not something you can rush through and hope to see results overnight. It doesn't work like that; it takes time. Building a brand also isn't just one thing. It's a culmination of many different things that come together. Not every single tip, trick, and approach dissected in this book will work for you and your business. You'll have to find what does work for you, lean into it, and disregard the rest. That will require trial and error, thought, preparation, and dedication. Buckle up!

What's Your Current Level of Visibility?

Don't fool yourself!

It's easy to think you're coming across one way online but that might not be how the outside world sees you. The best way to determine how the outside world sees you and the impression you make is to conduct a self-audit. You will have a digital brand, whether you put any effort into it or not. You might as well work hard to make sure it's creating an accurate impression and is an asset, not a detriment, to your business.

This audit is not intended to embarrass you. It's just

a hard look at what areas you need to improve on so you know where to begin the process. For the purpose of this exercise, you need to put your ego aside. Slip off your loafers and slide into your prospects' shoes. Try to experience what they experience and feel what they feel.

STEP #1: Write down five adjectives you want your brand to be recognized for.

You might use words like "professional," "caring," "experienced," or "capable." When people look you up online, what impression would you like them to have of you?

STEP #2: Why would someone want to work with you?

You don't have to go into much detail. Keep it to one or two sentences. You could say, for example, "I'm known for my professionalism and hard work, and my customers receive the best possible service."

STEP #3: Ask five to 10 people to go online, spend a couple minutes researching you, and tell you what they find.

The trick here is not to turn to your best friends or your family members. They already know you and have already formed an impression of you. Ideally, you want to ask someone who doesn't know you very well. Typically, a casual acquaintance will be less inclined to tell you what you want to hear, and more importantly, will also be more objective when judging only your online presence.

Step 4: Have the same five to 10 people complete steps one and two about you and your brand.

This can be an eye-opening and sometimes painful experience for some people. One of my managers sent the names of all her loan consultants to a good friend of hers in New York City who worked in advertising. She told him, "Pretend you were looking to get a mortgage and were referred to these people. Can you look them up online, go through this audit, and let me know what you think?"

The information she got back was incredible. One of her consultants wanted his brand to give the impression that he was professional, kind, and caring, but the feedback he got was that he looked like a "drunk idiot." One of her other consultants didn't even give the impression that he worked in mortgage. Rarely will a friend or family member be able to provide you with feedback that honest and valuable.

Before you go any further, your first priority is to clean up or remove any content from your current online profiles that doesn't fit your desired image. Remember that your brand, or reputation, is defined by anything you do. That includes everything from how you conduct yourself on the phone to what you wear. You don't want to overlook anything because it could be the reason why you're missing out on potential business opportunities. If you've had some comments about photos on your Facebook page of you drinking, it might be a good decision to get rid of them so they don't tarnish the online reputation you are trying to create. It's time to start controlling your image.

As bad as it could be, you can be thankful that you aren't in the same situation as a good friend of mine and fellow loan consultant. He has the same name as an ax murderer! Unfortunately, he has to put a little more effort into his brand because every time a potential customer Googles his name, guess what comes up?

Don't Worry, You Won't Become Famous

As I talk about the importance of building your brand, you may be thinking, *Hey Alec, I don't want to be famous. I don't need to be a weblebrity.*

Pause everything. Building your brand is not about being famous, going viral, or being popular to the masses. It's about having influence in your community and online and becoming a brand leader. The goal behind your effort is for you to be viewed as the local expert.

To show why building a brand is so important, I'll tell you the story of one of our loan consultants. During a training session, she told us, "I just realized my dad referred someone looking to get a loan to a loan consultant who wasn't me."

Everyone in the room groaned and was thinking the same thing: *Oh...your dad? That's gotta hurt.*

She knew it too, "Yeah, I guess I don't do a good enough job of letting people know that I'm great at what I do, looking for referrals, or even in the business at all."

That exchange is the single, best example of why you need to build an ecosystem that lets people in your community and online know who you are and what you do. If your branding is powerful and done right, whenever your friends, family members, pastor, bartender, and people of your community need to get a mortgage, they will think of you.

If you still have doubts, don't worry. I'll walk you through how to show up for your past and future customers in such a way that you will be recognized as the undeniable brand leader for what you do. You will see that building a brand has nothing to do with being famous or putting out overedited content that will change the world. Just because you start posting videos, that doesn't mean they will suddenly be retweeted by Ellen. Let's slow down.

CHAPTER 2

From Invisible to Visible

Did you know?

- Americans check their social media accounts 17 times a day.[1]

- Facebook has 2.07 billion monthly active users.[2]

- 500 million tweets are sent every day.[3]

- Instagram has 500 million daily users.[4]

Just having a Facebook page doesn't cut it anymore. You need to be on multiple platforms to ensure you're reaching the broadest audience possible. Someone right now is asking friends for professional service recommendations. Is your name on that list? Can those people tag you?

---

1 Irfan Ahmad, "Spanning the Decades: How to Market to Each Generation on Social Media (Infographic)," *Digital Information World*, November 11, 2016, https://www.digitalinformationworld.com/2016/11/infographic-marketing-each-generation-social-media.html.
2 Irfan Ahmad, "Spanning the Decades"...
3 Irfan Ahmad, "Spanning the Decades"...
4 https://www.omnicoreagency.com/instagram-statistics/.

Social Media Platforms

Each platform has its own voice, and you need to learn how to speak that voice from those platforms. Whether you need a primer or just a refresher, here is a quick rundown of the major platforms and how you can utilize them to build your brand and help your business become relevant and visible.

1. Facebook

Facebook is the most established social network with two billion daily active users. You may already have a personal account, and if you create a separate business page, you can use your existing network to gain followers. This doesn't mean that you can't use your personal account for business as well. You shouldn't bombard or overwhelm your friends and followers with work-related posts, but they should know that you're in mortgage. When on this platform, focus your efforts on sharing educational and engaging videos, blog posts, and curated content.

2. LinkedIn

Think of LinkedIn as your professional Rolodex and résumé with a profile that highlights your professional experience while allowing you to reach industry professionals, referral partners, and some clients. It has over

575 million users and 260 million active monthly users.[5] Make it a point to add new connections as you meet new people, especially referral partners and other industry professionals.

LinkedIn can be a valuable resource, but you'll want to use this network differently than you would Facebook or Instagram. It's specifically designed for business and professionals, which makes it a rich resource for prospects. When you position yourself as a mortgage expert, these decision-makers will typically come to you when they are searching for a lender or have any questions. You won't need to reach out to them directly if your content is doing its job. More on that later.

I know some salespeople avoid LinkedIn simply because they don't want to get harassed, spammed, and hounded by recruiters. If you are in sales, especially mortgages, I know you know what I am talking about. I understand any hesitation, but I guarantee you that you will find real estate prospects on LinkedIn. You're also likely to find customers and other business professionals on LinkedIn. I've watched LinkedIn transform into a preferred platform for adults. You can additionally try utilizing LinkedIn Pulse and various groups for establishing thought leadership and recruiting.

5 Osman, Maddy. "Mind-Blowing LinkedIn Statistics and Facts (2020)." *Kinsta. com/blog*. Last updated January 1, 2020.

3. Twitter

Think of Twitter as a microblogging service where users share short messages (tweets) at a rapid pace. It has 330 million users and 80 percent of them are mobile users.[6] This allows you to reach almost anyone and everyone.

You communicate on Twitter using tweets up to 280 characters long. If used correctly, Twitter has the power to be a great marketing tool for your business. To portray yourself professionally on the platform, it is crucial to make sure your handle, profile picture, header image, bio, and the first pinned tweet work cohesively and represent your business accurately. Focus on posting short, enticing content that creates trust. The key to success with Twitter is to create that trust with short content that leads to longer-format content.

4. Instagram

Instagram is a continuous feed of photographs, owned by and integrated with Facebook, and has over 1 billion users[7]. It allows you to reach clients, partners, large brands, and even celebrities. Since Instagram is owned by Facebook,

6 Aslam, Salman. "Twitter by the Numbers: Stats, Demographics & Fun Facts." *Omnicore blog.* Last updated September 5, 2019. https://www.omnicoreagency. com/twitter-statistics/.

7 Aslam, Salman. "Instagram by the Numbers: Stats, Demographics & Fun Facts." *Omnicore blog.* Last updated January 25, 2020. https://www.omnicoreagency. com/instagram-statistics/.

when you create an account, it will provide your Facebook friends as suggested people to follow. To gain a bigger following, you'll need to post engaging content and use tools such as tagging, hashtagging, and Instagram stories to further increase your reach. Be sure to research what your potential customers are hashtagging to make sure that your posts are going to be seen by the right people.

Instagram is a useful platform for targeting millennials. I know some millennial loan consultants who really leverage Instagram to build a brand. Keep in mind that Instagram is a lifestyle and culture platform so the strategy is very different. It's better suited for documenting than posting or campaigning, for example, but don't suddenly jump to a platform like Instagram if you don't regularly use it and don't know if you can reach your customers there.

5. YouTube

YouTube is the second largest search engine on the planet.[8] Besides memes and cat videos, you can also find hundreds of thousands of educational videos that engage consumers. It is likely one of the most important platforms where relevant professionals need to be. If you are not building a personally branded educational video series explaining what you do, why you do it, alongside the common ques-

---

8 "YouTube: The 2nd Largest Search Engine." *Mushroom Networks*, August 3, 2013. https://visual.ly/community/infographic/social-media/youtube-2nd-largest-search-engine.

tions and concerns of your customers, then you are 100 percent missing out. Additionally, YouTube is now a dominant search engine for nearly everything imaginable. It's a crucial place to show up!

The critical point is to go where your customers are. If your customers are on LinkedIn, that's where you should be. If they are on Facebook, that's where you should be. The more you post and the more you use these platforms, the more you'll know where to direct your attention. Make it a point to become fluent in the language of each platform because caption length, image formatting, and vocabulary differ from platform to platform. Don't simply post the same content on each platform; make sure you tweak how you communicate on each of these social channels. Think of how annoying it is when you see a post from someone on Facebook and then go to Instagram and see that the person has posted the same thing.

What's Your Digital Visibility?

It's okay if you're not yet on all the platforms or taking advantage of everything each one has to offer. The goal is to make tiny improvements organically over time to create a strong foundation to build off. But first, hone in on where you are today and perform a quick inventory of your active social channels and digital platforms.

- Facebook – How many followers? How many likes?

- LinkedIn – How many connections?

- Twitter – How many followers?

- Instagram – How many followers?

- Zillow/Yelp – How many reviews?

You may be familiar with these platforms but you may not know what to do with them or how to get started. You're not alone. If you weren't raised in the social media culture and are trying to learn this late in the game, it can be intimidating and confusing. Here is an eight-step guide to help you lay the groundwork.

#1. What Is Your Unique Value Proposition (UVP)?

The first step is figuring out what sets you apart. Why should people work with you? What's your message?

A key component of building a personal brand is knowing what you have to offer your audience. What are you giving them in exchange for their time and attention? You want to be able to articulate that clearly. For now, keep it simple. Boil down your message to one or two sentences. If your brand gets too scattered and you can't easily define it, then it will be hard to communicate it to your audience. It's so much easier to understand simple things.

For many people, this is harder than it seems, which is why I've created two checklists, internal and external, that can help you identify qualities that make you and your business unique.

Take your time. Answer the questions. There are no wrong answers, and nothing is permanent. This can change throughout the process and it probably will as you narrow your focus and figure out what works. But for the time being, these answers will help give you a starting point.

1. The Internal Checklist

Your Brand

- What makes you unique?
- What makes you smile, and why do you want to share it?
- How authentic are your conversations every day?

Your Values

- What values do you instill in your work every day?
- Why are these values important to you?
- How are these values demonstrated online?

Your Audience

- Who do you want to work with?
- What value do you bring to their lives?
- Where do you find them?

Your Vision

- Where is your brand going?
- How do you think your future feels?
- Have you made a plan to get there?

I know some of these questions are difficult to answer. If you're struggling, email a couple of your best friends and bounce some ideas off them to see what they think. They might not have all the answers for you, but it's an excellent way to get the ball rolling.

2. The External Checklist

Your Social Media

- First impressions are everything. What are your first impressions of your social media presence?
- Is your branding consistent across all your platforms?
- Are you participating in conversations or just observing?

Your Website

- Would you take *you* seriously?
- What is the point of your website, and how is it helping you grow your brand?
- Does your site encourage your visitors to want to seek your expertise?

Your Online Presence

- Are you well reviewed?
- Is the information you have in your heart and head online?
- Why would you do business with you?

Your Content

- Do you have modernized content that represents who you are today?
- Does your content represent success or does it represent sufficiency?
- Does the content you provide for your audience demonstrate your professionalism?

Next, think of three people in any industry who you admire or would like to emulate and Google them. Pay special attention to how they present themselves, what makes them unique, and how what you see makes you feel. Study other popular brands to see what kind of emotional response you get from looking at how they present themselves. What emotional response do you have to a brand like Apple, for example? Is it good or bad? Once you can pinpoint those traits, see if you can replicate them. What kind of response do you want your potential customers to have? Can you capture it?

Now that you've done some soul-searching and reflected on what works for other people and brands, take it all in and go back to see if you are better equipped to sum up your message, or your UVP, in one or two sentences.

If you want to see me doing my best to live out these examples, come hang with me on social media! Just use Google to find me on YouTube, Facebook, Instagram, Twitter, and TikTok.

#2. Understanding Your Market

You have a simple advantage on that online-lender call center. You know your community, the people in it, and what they care about better than an online lender who has probably never been there. You likely, if you work at a strong lender, have over 500 loan programs that you can offer a customer. That's a lot of knowledge for a lender to have. Would the lender in the call center know which one of those 500-plus programs would best fit that first-time homebuyer? Would the call center lender know of any local down-payment assistance programs that can give you

$10,000 in closing cost credit? You do because you live in this city. Knowledge like that can get overlooked. Use that to your advantage and look for ways to cater and position your brand to the needs of the customers you hope to serve.

Don't forget that you aren't the only one who does what you do in your community so this goes back to making yourself unique. Ask yourself the difficult questions that will help you stand out.

- What does my customer stand to gain from my service or product?
- How is my product different from those offered by competitors?

#3. Authenticity

You can't have a fake brand. People will smell it a mile away. The rub is that you can't actively promote yourself as being authentic—you are either authentic or you aren't. If you are posturing and not sharing authentically about who you are and what you stand for, people will not want to do business with you. Period.

Genuine authenticity happens when your words and actions align. So, for example, when you shake someone's hand, don't try to slip a business card into their pocket without being noticed. This can happen online as well. For example, has anyone ever connected with you on LinkedIn and then immediately tried to pitch you? How did that make you feel? Potential customers probably don't want to deal with that so you won't want to do it yourself to someone else.

Instead, try to be helpful, and you can do that by sharing content (which you will learn more about in chapter three) or your expertise without expecting anything in return. That is how you will ultimately be seen as genuine and authentic.

#4. Consistency

Consistency is essential in many ways. In an online presence, that means consistency in posting content, but it also means consistency in message or, for the lack of a better term, being on-brand.

I love Red Bull, for example, but I know that they don't sponsor dog shows. They sponsor action sporting events; that's their arena. They cater to customers who compete in and watch events where people skydive and jump out of spacecrafts.

In your business, consistency can also apply to clothing and how you dress. So many people overlook this, but the clothes you wear play an essential role in establishing your brand. You may want to present yourself as a five-star professional, which often means wearing a three-piece suit. If that's what you're going for, you won't want your online platforms to be loaded with photos of you at the beach. That's off-brand, and it can confuse your audience. To whom do you cater? Are you on-brand?

Growing your personal brand will gradually expand your presence across several marketing channels and social networks. As you create and optimize your social profiles, you will want to stay consistent in how you present yourself. Some basic tips will get you started so that you'll be easily identifiable and clearly defined:

- Use the same profile picture across all platforms.

- Use the same background and cover images across all platforms.

- Use the same color schemes across all platforms and promotional material.

- Dress consistently in your signature style, à la Steve Jobs or Mark Zuckerberg.

#5. Your Story

Who are you? Where do you come from? How did you get here? Why do you do what you do?

Those are all critical questions that make you who you are. I've come across so many people who are embarrassed about their story, be it their lack of education, where they came from, or how they see themselves in the mirror. But

I challenge you to lean in to your story. It's what makes you unique. It's also what makes you authentic and in the end, it will make you visible.

Everyone loves a good story. If you tell it well, it can become a powerful component of your brand. Storytelling is effective because it creates an emotional and human connection.

#6. Expertise

What's your niche?

Everybody should be known for something. For some lenders, it might be a knowledge of the process for first-time homebuyers. If that's you, build an online brand that reflects and incorporates your expertise. You'll want to leverage that expertise to show you are a pro. I know so many rock stars out there with 15 to 20 years of experience who are invisible to online users. They don't show off that experience so nothing shows up when you Google them.

#7. Visibility

You need to be visible for your audience to see you. That may sound shockingly simple but let me explain. What happens if you send a tweet and only have 20 followers? Probably nothing. That's not an effective tweet.

But it's not just about gaining followers. A good strategy

is to leverage the followers and contacts you already have in order to reach a broader audience. I have over 10,000 connections on LinkedIn, but let's say a recent article I posted on first-time homebuyers only got 450 views. That's terrible for the number of connections I have. What I could then do is reach out to my past customers and say something like, "I really care about first-time homebuyers. You all went through a process with me, and I hope it was as wonderful for you as it was me. If you know anyone who is a first-time homebuyer, please share this link with them."

You will be surprised by how well that can work. That's creating visibility, and it's not hard to do. Every time you want to make a post or create content, ask yourself if you will be visible and what you can do to make it visible. It's also a great way to draw more followers and views to your LinkedIn profile.

#8. Connections and Reviews

You are only as good as the people you know. Invite people to review, engage, and connect with you. Leverage your database of existing contacts to gain more contacts.

You don't want to get lazy or complacent. If you sit back and don't comment or engage in the digital sphere, it's like you're sitting in the corner facing the wall. You have to talk to people, share their content, and engage. One of the most powerful things that can happen to you is if a customer shares how wonderful you are with their contacts. "I closed a loan with Steve. He's amazing, and you should call this guy." That's a home run, but people are less likely to do that if you don't engage with them. It's a two-way street, so share their content, engage, and tag them. Invite them to your pages.

Not only will your connections help introduce you to others and expand your network, but they will also provide a growing list of testimonials that speak directly to your character. Testimonials and peer reviews are two of the strongest trust signals to customers who are considering doing business with you, which makes them invaluable. You can think of reviews like your credit score. Consumers take online reviews so seriously that 84 percent of them trust online reviews as much as they trust personal recommendations.[9]

To help you improve your credit score, use this effective 10-step checklist to getting quality online reviews:

1. **Do Good Work!** It's important to remember that good work leads to excellent reviews. Be open to feedback from the beginning of each transaction and mention early on that reviews help your business grow. Plant the seed.

---

9 Craig Bloem, "84 Percent of People Trust Online Reviews As Much As Friends…," *Inc.*, July 31, 2017, https://www.inc.com/craig-bloem/84-percent-of-people-trust-online-reviews-as-much-.html.

2. **Set Up Your Profiles.** Set up that Yelp page. If you don't have a place established for customers to leave reviews, you don't have any place where you can direct your customers to share posts.

3. **Be Considerate.** Your customers don't have to leave you a review. You're asking them for a favor so be nice when you approach them.

4. **Time It Right.** It sounds simple, but only ask for a review when you've had some success and you're positive any potential issues have been resolved. Don't ask at the closing table. Try to wait until the dust has settled, but don't wait too long either. You want reviews to have the customer's experience fresh in their mind.

5. **Just Ask!** This can be the most challenging part for some people. Remember that if you don't ask for reviews, you won't get them. If you don't want to ask in person or over the phone, send an email, but you have to ask.

6. **Be Specific.** Don't just ask for a review and assume that the customer knows what to do. Make it easy for them by providing a link so there is no confusion. Some customers may not be comfortable using those platforms and prefer instead to write a

thank you note. Ask if you can take a screenshot or picture of the note and post it to your social pages.

7. **Ask Again.** People are busy and people forget. If someone agreed to leave a review for you and has not followed through, politely reach back out and give them a gentle nudge as a reminder.

8. **Respond!** Post a response to the reviews you receive online. This not only sends an acknowledgment to the reviewer that you've seen their review but it also shows your other followers that you engage.

9. **Thank Reviewers.** Don't just respond on the social platform, make sure to thank your reviewers. Send a quick note, call, or text. Just let them know you're grateful. That can go a long way.

10. **Consistency Is Key.** There's that word again—consistency. Asking for and collecting reviews might be uncomfortable at first but as with everything else we've discussed, it will get easier and you'll figure out the best way to do it.

One question I get asked all the time is whether it's better to get reviews published on Yelp or Zillow. Remember that Zillow is a mortgage company, so I think of it like this: If Zillow decided tomorrow they were going all in on their own mortgage company, used only their own internal loan consultants, and wouldn't let outsiders market on their site, they could just turn off your page because they own it. And if you have 200 reviews on Zillow when they turn it off, that could be a massive blow to your business. That's why I would stay away from Zillow and go with Yelp. Yelp isn't owned by a mortgage company. There is a much better chance that they'll be around for a long time.

CHAPTER 3

Less Talk, More Action— For Real This Time

You can't suddenly become relevant without taking action. Digest everything you've learned this far and just do it. Don't put it off. Start tomorrow. No, start today.

You can do that by thinking of the acronym ICE:

> I – Identify
>
> C – Connect
>
> E – Engage

1. Identify

First, take the time to identify the people you want to connect with and include in your digital sphere. You can post all you want and have the best content of any expert in your area, but if you don't have many followers, you aren't going to drive results. I love getting comments from my mom, but it doesn't do me any good when it comes to expanding my business or building my brand.

When I ask people who they want to target, the most common answer I get is, "Everyone." That sounds good but everyone is not an audience. Start with past customers. Consider reaching out to real estate agents, home builders, influencers, business owners, friends, family, current homeowners, and potential new homebuyers. You'll want to seek out the industry players and influencers.

Once you've identified your audience, it will better help you to figure out which platforms to target, your posting schedule, the type of content you want to create, and the voice of your brand. I've seen too many people spin their wheels out of the gate because they weren't posting content that spoke to a defined audience. Spend time on this step so you can understand the unique challenges of your audience and what type of brands they already follow. This sort of competitive analysis can help you know how to help your own brand and social media presence stand out from the pack.

2. Connect

Next, come up with a plan for how to connect. The actual process is self-explanatory. Simply reach out to the people on your list. Surprisingly, many people fail to follow through and execute this step because they aren't intentional and they rely too much on a more organic system.

To avoid this mistake, take the time to develop a strategy and a schedule, and be sure to follow through. What platforms will you target? How often will you post? Maybe you set a goal for writing one article and posting one video every two weeks. Start small and commit to it. Create a content calendar to hold yourself accountable. I can't stress enough how important it is to stick with something that will work for you. It might be as easy as blocking out time every day. Depending on your schedule, you could devote 20 minutes in the morning to building your network and establishing your brand. Twenty minutes doesn't sound like a lot, but if you do that every single day, it will add up. It's a marathon, not a sprint, so consistency is what's most important here.

Many people come out of the gate hot and try to commit to writing too many articles and posting too many videos, and often their grand plan fails. Start small and build. Brands aren't developed by accident; they are developed with intentionality over time.

This is a step that should go on indefinitely. You'll want to stay active, so it's best to get used to it and make it a habit now. This is the equivalent of collecting business cards to add to your Rolodex. However, the trick to being effective is not to think of it as adding followers—think of it as building relationships. Follower counts have naturally evolved into a vanity metric but numbers alone don't do you any good. Having only 100 followers regularly communicate with you and your content is infinitely more valuable than having 10,000 followers who ignore you.

3. Engage

Finally, you'll want to engage. In basic terms, don't leave the "social" out of your social media presence. Send a Facebook profile request with a custom message. "Like" Instagram posts and give people a reason to follow you back. Tag people when posting the content that you create. Engage people with questions, comments, and likes. Always mention (@) the people you reference in your posts and reply when people mention you or share your content. Answer every question people ask you. Don't just like and retweet other people's content; reply with a comment and try starting a conversation. "Hey, remember me? We met a few months ago, and I was hoping to stay in touch. I hope everything is going well with your dog." Again, simple. Engage naturally instead of robotically. Engage like a human being.

Content Creation

Finally, it's time to talk about content. Content is what ultimately fuels the growth of your brand on social media. If you're coming into this cold and don't have experience creating content, let's start with the basics.

1. Writing Articles

I think one of the most underutilized platforms today is the LinkedIn article blog feature. You can write articles on LinkedIn and it will connect to your profile. Although many people think you need a blog, you don't actually need a blog. Your potential customers may not care about a blog, but they do care about relevant content. Write about what you care about. If you care about first-time homebuyers, you should write about how to protect yourself as a first-time homebuyer. You should show the world that you're an expert. If you share that content, it will come up in search feeds, allowing customers to find that content and identify it with you.

Don't assume that LinkedIn articles always need to be about business. When building up a brand, remember that it's important to come across as a normal human being with more than a professional life. When everything you do is work related and Uber Professional, you lose that human aspect. Customers want to do business with people they like. Writing articles and sharing content about life and the things you care about will make you authentic, unique, and most importantly, likable.

Sharing the personal details of my life was one way I built up my own brand. I posted content when I got married, bought my first house, and later got a dog. I'm not talking about sharing photos of the parties and crazy stuff but plain old human life.

If you want to share something personal, share something personal. We're in a social business that revolves around people. Not every post has to be roses. Life is not roses.

2. *Video Is King*

Creating your own YouTube channel is an unbelievable way to share content at a moment's notice so customers can find you. YouTube is the second-most popular search engine in the world, so your reach can extend even beyond your immediate followers. If someone goes on there to search for information about first-time homebuyers, your content can be made available to them. You can create videos in advance. Do a bunch in one day and then strategically release them so you can consistently post new content. That's a great way to build up a video library quickly.

The problem is that so few people want to branch out and do video because they are terrified. People are scared of how they'll look on video or they just flat-out don't know how to do it. The truth is that nobody knows how to do it until they do it. Another fact is that you will be terrible at making videos until you aren't. It's a skill. Nobody ever pushed the record button and started crushing amazing video content on their first try.

Eight years ago, I started a YouTube channel called *Drive Time with Alec*. When I got in my car, I put my phone on the dashboard and just recorded myself talking about whatever I wanted to talk about that day. I didn't have a script. It was all stream of consciousness, so I drifted into some random territory, and I was terrible at first. Many of those videos were awful, but I ended up doing 262 of them. And eventually, I got pretty damn good at making videos and being comfortable when talking to the camera. You just have to dive in and do it.

The reality is that most people watching these videos aren't going to care what you look like. Today, most online users are so focused on themselves that they aren't going to get out of their own heads. So you look foolish. Who cares? I compare those who are trying to build a brand to the people who make a New Year's resolution to go to the gym. Stereotypically, January gym-goers don't know how to use the machines; some of them might get on the machines backward. They're uncomfortable, and we can all tell they're uncomfortable, but that's okay because we've all been there. You are going to be one of those January gym-goers when you start out, and it's best to just accept that.

Do you remember the first cold call you made to a real estate agent? How awful was that? I'm still uncomfortable thinking of how I blew it and made myself look terrible, but I got a lot better. Don't worry about how you look. Focus on putting out authentic, consistent content that caters to a specific audience and what they want to learn about. The result will be unbelievable.

Another reason why so many people don't make this leap is that it brings up painful memories. Some of us can think back to when we started and had to go out into the wild world to find loans or else we didn't make any money. Four days a week, I used to drive around to open houses. I couldn't find them on the internet back then because they didn't exist on the internet yet. I'd walk into the open house and pitch myself to some real estate agent I didn't know. It was awful and probably on par with cold-calling people but I had to do it.

Trying to create a social media presence and building a brand is like going through those same growing pains all over again. So many veteran loan consultants don't want to put themselves through that discomfort again. Obviously, you don't have to do any of it, but you might not be in business much longer if you don't so the choice is yours.

If you're still not feeling motivated, try thinking about it like this. Salespeople make an effort to meet face-to-face with customers because they want to build a rapport. It's hard to do that over the phone or through email. When you see another person's face when speaking, you will have a deeper connection. You can see if the other person is paying attention. You can gauge their body language and facial expressions. It's something you do every day as a salesperson so you don't need to be scared to do that on video. Just turn your phone around, record yourself, put it up on Facebook, and suddenly you'll have 200 people paying attention to you. People are curious, and they will lock into it. To be blunt, you'll just need to get over yourself. If the ultimate goal is to meet face-to-face anyway, you're just doing it now instead of later.

If any of this feels uncomfortable, that's an excellent sign that you're doing the right stuff because success lies on the other side of fear. And what's so beautiful about video is that you can *delete* it. Just because you record something doesn't mean that you have to release it into the world. You can stop and start over any time you want—I do it constantly. Give yourself a break and don't put any pressure on yourself to nail a video on the first take. Try going off book or breaking with convention; it can lead to some surprising results you would never have discovered had you just stuck with the script.

Ditch the Gimmicks

Once I start talking about the importance of making a video, it isn't long before people start asking about editing, graphics, and music. I have the same answer to every one of those questions, "Don't worry about it. Just film!"

Be rough. Be raw. Be gritty. And above everything else, don't be scripted. The more authentic you are, the better. The number one video people will watch on your channel is most likely to be your blooper reel because it shows you're human and it's fun. People like to know that nobody is perfect. When you mess up on video, or say the wrong thing, it doesn't hurt you or your message; it actually helps you. It makes you appear relatable, which can improve your ability to establish genuine relationships while earning influence.

Before you get too carried away and completely throw caution to the wind, you'll want to make sure the basics are in order. Start by focusing on three areas.

1. **Sound:** Get a mic, test it, and listen to yourself. You may not like how you sound on video, but in this step, you're making sure the quality of the audio is clear so that people can actually hear you. Checking the sound is a very important step.

2. **Camera:** Where you put the camera is also something to consider. We've all seen those videos on

Instagram where people hold the camera under their chins, so we know how awful that looks and we won't want to do that! When it comes to the camera, up is good, down is bad. If you're filming on your phone, make sure your hands are steady. It's hard to watch a video when it looks like you're falling down the stairs.

3. **Light:** You don't need professional lighting, but make sure you have enough light so people can see you.

It's all common sense, really, but once the basics are in order, dive in and rock and roll. But before you get started, I have a little test, or a challenge, for you. It's not for you to go make a video. Nope. This is called the "cupcake challenge," and it's not about how many you can eat, so don't go there. Let's say you got an email from a colleague who wants you to film something fun that involves you getting a cupcake thrown in your face. What would you say?

The correct answer is yes. Not only do you want to do it but you want to lean into it. The point is that you can't take yourself too seriously. I firmly believe that is the key to happiness. Think about it. You don't have all the answers. You can't be perfect at everything you do. You can't know everything there is to know in the world. You know all of these things are true, so don't take yourself so seriously. Take off the armor. Relax. Self-deprecate every now and again to show people you aren't afraid to be vulnerable. I often catch myself taking myself too seriously and have to tell myself to chill out. Don't be afraid to put a sticky note on your computer to remind yourself to have a little more fun.

Relax. Go unscripted. Don't worry about graphics, music, or editing when you're starting out. Turn around the camera and hit record. And don't let anyone or anything stop you from being you or having fun. The more fun you have with this, the easier it will be and the better your videos will become because you will come across as an authentic person. Don't put so much pressure on yourself.

Pillar Content

Pillar content is a great way for you to create a ton of content, and now is the time to become familiar with this phrase if you haven't already done so.

The concept is simple. Pillar content is basically one lengthy piece of content, like a podcast or a keynote speech that you cut up into smaller, bite-size pieces and deliver to the world in installments. Think of all the material you could get from one of your keynote speeches. You can create short videos and photos with quotes to post on Instagram or little messages that you blast out on Twitter or Facebook. You can pull potentially 100 pieces of additional content from one keynote speech, so don't underestimate how powerful a piece of pillar content can be.

You may be saying, "But Alec, I don't do keynotes." That is totally fine, but that doesn't mean you don't have other content you can use as pillar content. Think about what you could utilize instead. For example, you may do an hour-long lunch-and-learn. If so, film it! That becomes your keynote. That is your piece of pillar content that you can then cut up a million different ways. Once you start looking for those sources of potential pillar content, you will be surprised to find there are more opportunities out there than you realize. Once you get thinking like that, it will make content creation so much easier. In fact, try to create one piece of pillar content every quarter.

Don't Be Boring, Don't Be Predictable!

You'll want to start your content creation by writing articles and posting videos, but if that's all the content you create, eventually your audience will tune out. Another problem that people have right out of the gate is that they run out of ideas and end up posting content that grows repetitive or is a different variation of the same thing. Get creative. Think outside of the box. Look for different ways to engage. Not all of these ideas will work for you or your business, but if you get stuck, look over this list and see if it inspires any new approaches.

Employee News

Highlighting new employees at your office shows your network that your company is made up of real people. It doesn't even have to be a new employee. Do you have a rock star assistant who goes above and behind? Post a photo. Tell a story.

Company News

Please don't feel the need to provide an update for every new product, program, or meeting happening in your company because that is a good way to lose followers. But don't be afraid to share exciting updates or a new loan product.

Client Closing

If you attend a closing, snap a photo to post, but be respectful and remember that it's the client's moment. It's not always about you!

Community Event

Remember to be human instead of robotic, and humans remain active in their communities. You might work a car wash to raise money for your kid's soccer team so that they can purchase new uniforms, for example. Post photos and let people know what's going on.

Events

Obviously, if you're hosting or attending an industry-related event, be sure to snap some pictures and share them.

Local Businesses or Professionals

Remember how it's not always about you? If you scratch someone else's back, they'll scratch yours, so share the content and pages of your local network of business partners. Share recommendations; it portrays you as a local expert and shows that you support other local businesses.

Holiday Messages

A lot happens around the holidays. Document it and post it, but remember to keep it PG. You don't want to go off-brand or create a bad impression of yourself.

Real Estate and Mortgage News

You will find no shortage of industry news. There are so many articles and videos out there to share but that's what everyone is doing. You'll want to take that a step further. Don't just share a video but try to add a fresh new perspective on the news. What's your opinion about what's going on? A study from IDC Research shows that 80 percent of smartphone users check their phones within 15 minutes of waking up.[10] Take advantage of that and position yourself as a market expert by posting early. If you are the first one to share the news that day, your followers are likely to get those updates from you.

Earn Some Headspace

To understand what headspace is, think about all those funny Geico commercials or the Super Bowl ads you see every year. What are those companies doing? Yes, they are advertising and paying a lot of money to do so. But whether you know it or not, they are also earning a space in your brain, so when you need something, their brand comes to mind. This isn't a technique reserved for big Fortune 500 companies with deep pockets to spend on advertising. Without spending a dime, you can implement an equation that will get you ahead and help you earn that headspace in your customer's brain.

You have had customers in the past; you took care of them and you loved them. But since you closed their loans, you perhaps only communicate with them by occasionally sending them a crappy drip email. Now they've forgotten all about you. You've lost that headspace. Just because you

---

10 Pickhan, Ryan. "80% of Smartphone Users Check Their Phones Before Brushing Their Teeth ... And Other Hot Topics," *Constant Contact blog*, accessed January 15, 2020.

send them an email that they won't read, it doesn't mean that you're on their brain.

When I speak to a group of new hires, I ask how many of them have over 10,000 unread emails in their inbox right now. Half the people in the room raise their hands. This tells me that there are two types of people in the world—those with over 10,000 unread emails and those who have zero. There is no in between. Chances are that your drip campaign emails are only some of the 10,000 sitting in someone's inbox or they are immediately deleted. Either way, they aren't driving anything home.

Even if you follow every piece of advice, film a ton of videos, and put out consistent content, you still run the risk of all that content turning into white noise. It's no fault of your own. Think about how many times you just sit there, scrolling through your feed. You see videos and just keep scrolling right past them. That probably happens a lot. And you've probably missed a lot of great videos, just like so many people have missed some of your great videos. So what do you do about it?

Here's the magic equation. When you're playing the high-level content creation game and sending out information to the masses, you have to take the time to pull back and go directly to the customers. Let me give you an example. I know a guy named Mike who is a rock star for a really cool tech company. We met at a digital marketing conference, hooked up on social media, and rarely ever talked again. I'd see his posts but never paid much attention. Then one day, he sent me a personal note, "Alec, keep up the good videos. I'll reach out next time I'm in the area." He didn't just send a note. He also sent me a bunch of kick-ass stickers that went great with one of my campaigns. Now Mike has headspace in my brain, and every time one of his posts pops up in my feed, I think about how great of a guy he is and check out what he's doing.

Here's another example: I connected with a local real estate agent on Facebook. Just like Mike, this real estate agent got lost in my sea of connections until he did something unique, and it happened on my birthday. (Yay, my birthday is in August!) I received numerous generic messages but that real estate agent stood out. He was the only person to turn his camera around, hit record, and send me a video on Facebook that said, "Hey Alec, I saw it was your birthday. Just want to wish you a happy birthday and I hope you have a great day."

That was it. Done. No pitch. No "click here." No "let's set up a meeting." But now, every time I see him pop up in my social media feed, something clicks in my head. I barely know him but I think of him as a good guy, and he's got a little more headspace in my brain because he took 10 extra seconds to send me that personalized video on my birthday.

That's the equation. That's the magic trick. It's about being unique and not falling into the trap of doing what everyone else is doing on social media because it's so easy to blend in with the wallpaper. The harsh reality is that you will never get that Super Bowl commercial but you can do something way more impactful. You can have personalized interactions and engage with people to show them that they matter and are important. Take the time to break the mold and do something different and you will earn yourself a little more headspace in the minds of those you're trying to win over.

Do People Like You?

It should go without saying that when you occupy headspace in a person's brain that it should be for a good reason. You want people to like you. It sounds simple but sometimes this is easier said than done.

There is one universal truth that has been the same since I was starting out and going belly-to-belly with real estate agents in the streets on the weekends. The battlefield may be changing and moving online but the sales process and the way you build influence remains the exact same. It can be boiled down to three steps: likability, credibility, then opportunity.

The first step is that you have to be likable. The likability factor is crucial because if people don't like you, they aren't going to want to work with you. Real estate agents won't want to refer customers to you. Before anybody cares if you're good at your job, they will first decide if they like you. Think about that when making your videos and crafting your brand. You want to make sure you're presenting yourself in a way that is approachable.

Too many people make the mistake of trying to get right to the sale without worrying about being likable. When you skip that first step, you make it almost impossible to forge any kind of genuine relationship and you may never earn that seat at the table. Once you've addressed the likability factor, then you can focus on credibility and opportunity, but don't be so quick to Jerry Maguire it and go after the quick close.

Consistency Trumps Content

It's more important to be consistent than it is to put out tremendous content.

Think about the way social media works. You can have all the contacts and followers you desire but how many of them do you think will scroll through their feeds and stop to watch your video? I'm sure that many people haven't watched all of my videos, and a good share probably haven't seen a single one. That's okay. I'm perfectly fine with that. However, I bet those same people recognize my face—smiley or weird—because they're used to seeing it pop up in their feed. What can that tell you?

Don't spend hours trying to craft the perfect piece of content and then sit back expecting it to make a splash if it means that you can't post consistently. Sure, if you can post good content consistently, you can win every time, but when starting out most people tend to lean in one direction or the other. I'm not saying you should put out garbage just to make sure you post consistently, but there is an ancillary benefit to what I'm suggesting. What you will quickly understand is that the more consistently you make and post content, the better you will get at it. It's just like practicing your free throws—the more you shoot every day, a better shooter you will become. It's the same thing with content creation.

If you happen to catch yourself overthinking or obsessing meticulously over your content, just remember: Chances are good that most of the people in your orbit aren't even paying that much attention. That's why you want to have fun with it and just do what you do.

As important as all of this is, don't lose sight of the fact that your brand is not your salvation. The best branding in the world is meaningless if you don't have the talent and the drive to back it up. You can be a great basketball player and a deadly three-point shooter but you don't have a chance of making it to the NBA if you can't play defense. Remember what got you here and what made you successful. Think of your brand as a complementary, but necessary, skill set that must be built on top of your foundation.

PART II

DIGITAL MARKETING

CHAPTER 4

Stop Posting, Start Campaigning

Y ou will need to know the difference between marketing and branding.

People often assume branding and marketing are the same thing or mistake one for the other but they are very different. Branding is about who you are and how you want to be seen. Branding draws attention to your efforts. You can think of it this way: If you go to the gym wearing a T-shirt for the company where you work, that's branding. Now people know where you work but that does very little on its own. Nobody is coming up to you and saying, "I was going to get a loan, and then I saw your shirt. Let's do this thing!" If that does happen, more power to you, but for most people, business comes to fruition because of your marketing campaigns.

Think of it another way: If you put together a local marketing campaign, you will simultaneously brand yourself but it doesn't work the other way around. Branding will not generate marketing for you because branding alone is not tied to a result. It's like posting on social media. Posting is great. Yes, you want to post, and there are so many people out there who use social media only to post. "Hey, look! Here's my favorite cat video. It's awesome!" Who doesn't love that? Some of those videos are phenomenal but what kind of results are you getting? How does it impact your business? Don't get caught in the trap of pointless posting. If you find yourself frequently making those types of posts, you'll want to do a gut check because you're only doing the equivalent of wearing a company T-shirt to the gym.

Let's recap. You've identified your audience, gained followers, and developed a connection with those followers so now it's time to be active and alive. It's time to narrow your focus so you can put content out there that creates leads and gets results. That's the entire point of this, right?

Arguably, one of the best ways to do that is by developing a **campaign**.

Simply put, a campaign is a social media strategy with the intended purpose of acquiring potential customers who need your services. Think about political campaigns: Their objective is crystal clear. Their entire purpose is to get you to vote for a candidate or a proposition. Your campaigns should be no different. You want people to turn to you for your professional services or to refer you to others who require those services.

It all starts with a topic but it can't just be any old topic. You want to pick something you're passionate about because the first thing you will need to do for your audience is to establish your "why." That passion needs to be authentic or you risk losing your audience. As you've learned, you can't fake authenticity. You must pick a campaign idea you care about and that you're knowledgeable about because you need to show why you're the expert. Following are some ideas.

Campaign Topic #1: Protecting the First-Time Homebuyer

We've talked about this topic a lot already, so let's run with it and use it as the basis for a sample campaign that I can walk you through.

Once you come up with your campaign topic, you need to establish your "why." Why do you want to protect first-time homebuyers? Why are you passionate about this topic? What makes you the expert?

If you're pre-crisis like me, you've seen people lose their homes. You've seen people make lousy financial decisions and take loans that weren't good for them. You probably have friends and family who were impacted by this. All of this can provide you with a good foundation that will help you put together a campaign geared toward protecting and educating the first-time homebuyer.

Once you establish that why, you can start building your campaign, and the first step is to gather as much information as possible. This will be the material you will draw from when crafting content. Lay out the crucial steps every first-time homebuyer will need to know going into the process. Think about the critical questions first-time homebuyers typically ask. Here are some topics and sample questions to get you thinking.

- Why is it so important to review your credit, and what is the best way to do it?

- What documents do you need to get in order? Do you have your pay stubs, tax forms, driver's license, identification, and bank statements?

- What can you afford? How can you take an inventory of your income, savings, and debts to determine how much you can put toward a down payment, and how much you can afford to pay each month?

- What are the components that make up your monthly mortgage payment? How much do you know about the principal, interest, taxes, and insurance?

- Do you know your DTI, or debt-to-income ratio? Your DTI is what underwriters look at when determining your ability to repay your mortgage.

- How does the preapproval process work, and what should you look out for?

- What do you need to know before you apply, and how do you correctly fill out a Uniform Residential Loan Application?

- What's involved in getting an appraisal, and how is that different from an inspection?

- What is a purchase and sales agreement?

- How do you properly prepare to submit your loan application to the underwriter?

- What do you do if your mortgage application gets denied?

- What is "clear to close" and how is it issued?

- How do you correctly fill out your closing documents?

If you're stuck or short on ideas, go back and look at

all the flyers your company has on this topic. As you pick apart each one, I guarantee you will find 20 to 30 topics. Try using a whiteboard or an Excel spreadsheet to keep track of everything. You obviously don't have to include every single detail in your campaign. You don't want to bombard your audience with too much information because that would be counterproductive. The point is, you can find plenty of information that you can use when creating content, but it's not all about facts.

Don't underestimate the power of past experiences and storytelling when rolling out a campaign. What success stories have you heard or witnessed that can influence and inspire those looking to buy their first home? What cautionary tales have you heard or seen that can help new homebuyers avoid making the same mistakes? List all stories that can be used as part of your campaign, because those stories will put your customer in the shoes of someone who has been through it all before. Arguably, there is no better teacher than the successes and failures of others. You can always *tell* someone about the potential pitfalls and common mistakes but to *show* how this all goes down in the real world really hammers the point home in a way that facts can't.

What's the Goal of Your Campaign?

Your obvious goal is to increase your visibility and gain customers but specifically, you also want the campaign itself to have a goal. Before you design your campaign, you want to know that goal so you can incorporate it into the content and build toward that objective.

So for our first-time homebuyer campaign, what do we want to build toward? There are many different avenues you can take, but one relevant and straightforward way to end the campaign is by hosting a first-time homebuyer seminar in the hopes of attracting 25 people to the event. Done the right way, seminars can be a valuable client and lead-generating vehicle. They've become the go-to marketing tool in our industry, but the key phrase is "done right" because they do require some thought and preparation.

First, you'll want to find a venue. Venues can vary depending on your community, target audience, connections, and budget. You can rent out a conference space in a hotel or a library. You could plan to meet at a local restaurant. Whatever the location, plan ahead, and make sure the necessary arrangements are in place.

Once you have the event locked down, set up a page on a site like Eventbrite so that you can easily provide details for the event and send out invites when ready. You'll want the page to look good and contain all the necessary information because you're going to be referencing and directing people to this page throughout your campaign. You also want to make sure you collect all attendee info for the event so you can follow up afterward and arrange to send everyone home with all the necessary supplemental material you will be providing at the event. SPOILER ALERT: I will be doing a deep dive into this topic in the next part so hold your questions until then.

What's Your Strategy?

A lot of people want us to hand them a cookie-cutter campaign but it doesn't work like that and that approach typically lacks authenticity. Also, everyone is different, starting at a different level, and has a different audience. We all have different bandwidth for the amount of content we can create so you must create a strategy specific to you and your campaign.

There is a sweet spot when it comes to how often you campaign and the frequency with which you post. A good rule of thumb is to post as frequently as you can while maintaining your authenticity *and* while making sure that your content is fresh. If that means one video every Friday, then that's what you do. If your bandwidth for creating videos is one every month, start doing that and try to increase the frequency as you become more comfortable. Take baby steps if you have to. It's better than nothing.

Don't focus immediately on frequency but on quality and purpose. If your content is strong, helpful, and well-received, then your campaign can be effective. If you can't put out videos as often as you'd like, use your other social media outlets as additional lanes of traffic to drive people to your post.

Also, keep in mind that you can do too much. Posting multiple videos multiple times a day can be overwhelming. There is something called social media overkill, especially if you suddenly go from posting zero videos a week to 12. That can be jarring for your audience and chances are your customers will get annoyed if they see you posting all the time. That doesn't mean there aren't people out there who will love that approach and be super connected to it but if you annoy your customers, you aren't off to a good start.

When you're starting out, you want to find a balance. Most people keep it between three and five posts per week. Make sure you switch it up so you're putting out different content. You don't want to only make videos, only write articles, or only send out tweets. Don't lull your audience to sleep. Be creative and unpredictable.

To recap, here's your plan: For your first-time homebuyer campaign, you're going to come up with a six-week plan, which will involve posting one video every week along with multiple articles and FAQ pages for first-time homebuyers, culminating in a seminar at the local community center where you hope to have 25 people attend. Easy, right?

Making the Videos

Don't underestimate how powerful it is to put your face, voice, and message front and center on a video. Videos are the most personal, memorable, and eye-catching content for your potential audience. Plus, you're talking directly to your audience. Customers want to see the real you; they don't want to see your assistant or get some kind of flyer or auto-post. Videos are the best way, short of a face-to-face conversation, to get potential customers to recognize and like you so videos should serve as the foundation of your campaign.

For the purposes of your campaign, you'll need six videos so that you can post one video each week. Go back to that whiteboard or Excel spreadsheet and start sifting through the ideas that will make for the best video content. You may be releasing only one video every week but nowhere does it say that you have to wait a week before making the actual video. You can sit down and make all of them at once and knock them all out relatively quickly. Just be clever: Don't wear the same clothes, sit in the same location, or make it look like you've filmed them all at the same time. Spice it up!

Keep the videos short and listen to what your audience

tells you. Facebook right now is saying that videos should be three minutes but pay attention to how long they are actually being viewed. Few people will want to watch super long videos. The purpose is to raise awareness, attract potential customers, and promote your upcoming event. You can do that in a video that's one minute long.

You'll want every video to be unique. It should provide different information and it should be personalized. Unique, personalized material will generate more results when compared to the boring, preapproved generic content. Generic content can be useful in a different capacity, but you want to utilize these videos to draw in customers by being authentic, entertaining, likable, and knowledgeable. Make sure that it's organic but thoughtful.

The type of video content you decide to put out depends on a lot of different factors like your personality and comfort zone with videos, but here are six potential video ideas for your sample six-week campaign for first-time homebuyers.

Video #1: Start with your why. It's important that you know your why and that your customer knows it as well. They need to trust you, and they need to know the reason behind your passion before they give you their business. You can't fake authenticity so speak from the heart. Get personal if you have to.

Video #2: Customer testimonials can be powerful and work well on video. Film one with a former customer whom you helped out and let that person talk about how great you are. "Yeah, Alec helped me with the loan, and it was awesome! I didn't even know that I could afford it until he came along." Remember that not every customer will be up for this but that doesn't mean that they can't help out. They can leave you a review on Zillow, Yelp, or Facebook. Utilize it all!

Video #3: Pick a topic. You can choose from those listed earlier in this chapter. When you're dealing with first-time homebuyers, what questions do they most frequently ask? What are the common mistakes to avoid? What is the single-most beneficial thing a first-time homebuyer should know going into the process? There is no wrong answer. You might just take a video to talk through the process. Find a topic and make it the subject of your next video.

Video #4: Bring in an expert from another field. It might be a real estate agent who can offer his or her insight into another aspect of the process. Maybe you're friends with an underwriter who can talk about how to structure a deal. What are the questions they typically get? Are there any common misconceptions? What piece of advice would that pro give to first-time homebuyers? Give your audience a peek behind the curtain.

Video #5: Interview a former first-time homebuyer who

has already gone through the process. This can put your target audience in the shoes of someone who has been there. Have them share their story. Their point of view and advice might be slightly different from yours. It's a different perspective. Just make sure that the topics being discussed are different so you aren't creating videos that tell your audience the same thing a different way. You want these videos to provide a well-rounded but brief tutorial for first-time homebuyers with many insights and points of view.

Video #6: Promote your event. Remind everyone what you're doing at the end of these six weeks. If you only have 10 people who have committed to attending, ask for help in getting another 10. Ask for people to spread the word and share your content.

When making these videos, or any videos for that matter, don't forget to keep it casual. You're obviously doing this for a purpose and you want to share your expertise but you also want to be loose. If you just sit there and read a script, you will put your audience to sleep. Have fun with it. Let your personality shine. Be yourself because you don't want these videos to come off like a sales pitch or a commercial. It doesn't matter what you're selling; customers hate being marketed to. More than anything, customers want a relationship. They want an experience that adds something to their hectic lives, and it always comes back to authenticity. Authenticity is the secret sauce that separates the transactional experience (money in exchange for a service with no emotional connection) from the relationship experience.

Supplemental Content and Follow-Through

If you need to, flip back to the last part to remind yourself how each social media platform should be considered a different medium. If you're creating videos to post on Facebook or your YouTube channel, you want to keep them short because that's how people typically digest that content. It prevents you from going into too much detail about a specific topic but that's okay because you have other outlets and mediums in your arsenal.

You could supplement with an article. If you have a lot of insight and information about one of those topics related to first-time homebuyers, consider writing a LinkedIn blog post. If you're comfortable writing articles, try working that into the campaign. Maybe on Fridays you post a video on Facebook and every Tuesday you post an article on LinkedIn. That expands the scope of your campaign while also targeting a different audience.

Don't stop with LinkedIn. Utilize Twitter to provide links to your videos, articles, and upcoming events. Link other articles on the subject matter and encourage your followers to comment. Try to start a conversation and get the opinions of others.

Every part of the campaign is connected so tie it all together. Make sure you provide links to your website in all of your posts. Make your email address and phone number readily available in all of your posts so potential customers can contact you. All the while, you'll want to engage with your followers by liking their posts and commenting on their content. Ask others to share your content with someone who may benefit from it. Don't forget that everyone who views, shares, or tags one of your posts is someone you should add to your database for follow-up later because there might be an opportunity there.

If you feel like you might have trouble keeping up or staying on target when it comes to creating and posting content, plan ahead. Block out a certain amount of time each week or day to devote to your campaign and content creation. Put it in your calendar. This stuff works but you have to make the time to do it.

CHAPTER 5

Guideposts for Campaign Success

I f you're new to all of this, keep in mind that you may not get the results you want right away. I'm not trying to discourage you but it's just the harsh reality. Rarely does someone knock it out of the park during their first time at bat. This is a skill that requires practice, but the more you do it and the more comfortable you become in the digital space, the better you'll get. However, even if you get just one person to show up at your event, that's not a failure. That made all of your work worth it. That's one person who is talking to you about buying a home and it's one more potential customer than you had before you started. It's exactly what you wanted.

Yes, embrace even the smallest victories but continue to learn and improve. If you're getting low turnout at events, or no turnout at all, take a closer look at your content and your approach to make sure you are doing everything possible to become more visible:

- Is your audience big enough?
- Are you utilizing the right platforms to reach your target audience?
- Are you connecting with the right people?
- Is your content relevant?
- How much engagement are your posts getting?

We're all human. We're all going to make mistakes but you have to be honest with yourself. Figure out what you did wrong. Find the area where you need to improve and focus on that. It's all part of the process and the process is always evolving. Just keep at it. Continue to like, respond, and contribute. Continue to build your audience and create content. You're getting yourself out there and learning how to market yourself as the go-to expert, which is the most important thing. It's all about the long game and planting seeds because you never know which ones will grow.

One problem I've seen often is that people run their campaign from their Facebook business page but they don't have people liking and following the posts from that page. In many cases, not enough people are connected to the business page. This is a time when you want to cross-post by directing those on your personal page to your business page. As you've learned before, you don't just want to repost the same thing because that will come across like it's stacked on people's feeds and that can be annoying. Instead, engage with those on your personal page for a specific purpose and reason. Reach out. Ask for help. Don't ever be afraid to ask for help. That's how this works, and when the time comes, you can return the favor.

So many people get caught up in the social media aspect of marketing and campaigning. It's been the focus of the previous two chapters, but don't become so singularly focused that you lose sight of the bigger picture or what has been effective in the past. Don't forget that you have an entire database of contacts you can reach out to. Direct mail strategies and traditional ways of marketing still exist and can be incredibly powerful if done correctly. It doesn't hurt to branch out if your campaign needs a bump. You want to stay committed and stay consistent, but you can get creative in the ways you go about doing that.

How Often Should You Campaign?

Stick to one campaign at a time. If you try to run multiple campaigns at the same time, it can be overwhelming and confuse your audience. If the community and your followers want to help you, running numerous campaigns can put you in competition with yourself for their attention.

You also don't want to reuse old campaigns. You can

run a future campaign on a reused topic. You will never run out of first-time homebuyers. They will always exist, they will always have questions, and they will always need guidance through the process (which also continues to evolve) so you'll want to continue to target that ever-changing audience. However, you don't want to do so with the same campaign and same content.

If you're going to create content for a topic you've already created a campaign around, you'll want to come at it from a fresh, new approach. Make sure it looks different. Make sure you look different in the videos. There are plenty of topics out there for you to cover and a plethora of material you can use as the basis for your content. Spice it up because social media can get stale. Few people will connect with dated material they've already seen.

The Power of Digital Campaigns

If you're new to the digital sphere, this can be overwhelming but it's okay. Be overwhelmed! It will get you thinking and taking baby steps in the right direction.

Fall back on traditional marketing methods if you need a boost but don't get lazy. Remember that mailers can be a good way to get attention but they also cost money. Digital campaigns are a completely different beast and are by far the most cost-effective way to become visible to a broad audience. You have hundreds, if not thousands, of people in your market you can reach for free. It only costs you your time and the ability to endure the learning curve, which means that your ROI could be limitless. It's also possible to track all of this. You can better understand your demographics when running a digital campaign than you ever could before.

The more content you post, the more you might realize that some aspects of social media marketing will come to you more naturally than others. You might find you're better at writing articles than you are at making videos. You might get more of a response on Facebook than Twitter. That's all natural, but the beauty of digital campaigns is that it doesn't say anywhere that you have to do it alone.

You might have a coworker, colleague, or acquaintance in an entirely different industry who is good at the things you struggle with. If that's the case, team up, work together, and help each other out. That can be the nudge you need to get out of your digital comfort zone to expand the scope of your audience and, in turn, the potential audience you can reach.

The idea might come up to try to outsource some of this work. Many people want to try to outsource their own jobs and still get paid. However, if someone is doing the bulk of the work for you, you are massively at risk. I will give you one crucial piece of advice: I would strongly argue that outsourcing digital marketing is a mistake. I believe it causes you to lose your authentic voice. If you learn the skills and do the work yourself, you will be better for it in the end.

You are most likely reading this book for a reason. You're either an experienced professional who has lost business or is merely looking to learn more about the modern digital world to expand your business. Either way, realize that the customers you need to reach and the connections you need to make are currently outside of your comfort zone so sooner or later you will have to take the leap if you want to see the results.

Plan Ahead

You don't always have to be running a campaign. A little time in between campaigns can give your audience some room to breathe, but that doesn't mean you can't be thinking toward the future. Plan out campaign ideas for the rest of the year. The more planning you do ahead of time, the smoother the posting and campaigns will go because you've worked out the kinks. You don't have to know everything right out of the gate. Just do exactly what you did before and start with a topic you're passionate about. Here are a couple more examples.

Campaign Topic #2: Educating Our Veterans

What's your why?

Educating our veterans is another good topic to be passionate about. If you're a veteran yourself, or if you have family and friends who are vets, that can be your why right there. Let your audience know that you want to educate veterans on how to use their VA benefits to buy a home because most don't know how to use it, what it provides, or how they can take advantage of it.

What are some topic ideas that you can turn into content?

- How VA renovation works for vets and disabled vets.
- A video about your why. Why do you care about vets?
- Interview a veteran you helped close on their home.
- Explain the VA benefits that potential homebuyers can take advantage of.
- Talk about how to write a strong offer with VA financing.

Come up with 20 different ideas, but you don't have to think of them all yourself. Speak to friends and reach out to veterans to get the lay of the land. In other words, step into the space yourself so you can become a more educated expert.

What's your goal for the campaign?

For this particular campaign, your goal might be to educate 10 vets about VA home buying. That's a powerful result that you can tie into your campaign posts. Remind people. Ask for help and referrals so you can connect with those vets in your community who can benefit from your expertise.

Campaign Topic #3: The Power of Reno

Home improvement and fixer-upper shows are everywhere on television today, and that should be a good indication that there is a market out there interested in this topic. It's a massive trend in entertainment, housing, and financing. You can become that local expert in your community that an audience can turn to for answers.

But how will those in your area looking to renovate their homes know to turn to you? They will know because you can put together a badass campaign with a far-extending reach that will bring you to their attention. That campaign also has the potential to make you likable, which immediately gives you a leg up on the competition. With a well-established social media presence, a quick Google search will reinforce that belief and possibly make you their first phone call. As it begins to work, you will better see the power of becoming more visible.

A few years ago, loanDepot pioneered the VA Renovation Loan, and a few companies have followed suit, because it is such an amazing product for veterans who have served our country and deserve a perk. This loan offers a ton of guideline flexibility, underwriting flexibility, and down-payment flexibility up to zero. Plus, they can add a renovation benefit into it.

When we buy a house, we know that we'll likely spend $20,000–$30,000 just to get in there. It costs money; no house is perfect and repairs need to be done. Some of our disabled vets can afford the house but can't afford to make it accessible. Many resources and nonprofits can help vets, but the unlimited VA Renovation Loan can provide extra cash to put in a ramp, widen a doorway, or retrofit a kitchen.

If you're ever speaking to a group of people and ask them how many have served our country in the military, you will see a bunch of hands go up. Then if you ask how many of them have family members who have served, you will see about 70 percent of the hands go up in the room. We are all surrounded by veterans, but few are familiar with the VA Renovation Loan. This particular loan may not be for every vet, but it's your job to tell the vets in your community about it. Share the resources you have and serve the people who have served us. An unlimited veteran renovation loan for a disabled vet could be the most rewarding loan you do all year.

Digital campaigning can be a powerful tool in your arsenal but there is a rub: You have to be passionate about the topic you choose. This is where authenticity comes back into play. The other thing that's important to consider is your individual market. Home repair and renovation may be extremely popular on the national level but if there isn't much demand for it in your market, don't bother making it the basis of your campaign. It's the same with veteran benefits. You want to make sure that you're focusing your efforts not only on what you care about but also on what your potential customers care about. If you aren't, find out what they do care about, make it your passion, and become that expert.

PART III

LOCAL
MARKETING

CHAPTER 6

Become a Local Legend in Your Community

While creating your brand, increasing your influence, and crafting effective campaigns to become visible once again, don't lose sight of where you can be most effective—your local community.

I've watched too many loan consultants get so wrapped up in social media that they completely forget about what's happening outside their own office door. As important as it is to build your online presence, don't let that come at the detriment of the real-life benefits that you and your business could have from human interaction in your own community. Throughout this entire process, you'll want to establish those local relationships in the hope of generating real customer opportunities. That requires making a local marketing plan one of the foundational tentpoles of your business strategy. Becoming a known and trusted professional in your community puts you in a position that no online lender can duplicate, but it also allows you to reach the potential customer first. In today's competitive and cutthroat environment, getting there first is half the battle.

I don't mean that you need to plaster your face on bus stop benches and shopping carts; I'm suggesting that you support and engage with your community through authenticity, education, and service to increase your influence as a mortgage professional. Your local community is where you live, go to church, workout, go out to eat, and take your kids to various sporting events. It's where you're known. If you aren't known, you should be because there is an opportunity right on your doorstep that no ad or social media feed can replicate.

What's Your Level of Visibility?

By this point, you should notice that much of what's being discussed here is connected and it almost always begins with you and what you're passionate about. That's how you can personalize your efforts, create impact, and add value. Start by asking yourself two questions:

#1. What do I care about?

Clearly, you can't make something the focus of your local marketing efforts if you don't care about it. In other words, if you don't care about running, don't support a local 5K. People will notice your apathy and it will come across as inauthentic. Why would anybody want to waste their time participating in something that you, the person who is organizing the event, don't even care about? But if you *are* a runner, a 5K could be the perfect opportunity for you.

#2. What does my local market care about?

You have to consider how the people in your community feel about your idea because they are your target market.

For example, I grew up playing volleyball. I even played in college. When I meet people who grew up somewhere else, some of them have no idea that men could even play volleyball in college, so I have to tell them, "Yes, men do play volleyball, and the shorts are very comfortable." Still, when I talk about volleyball, those people can't relate because it's not popular where they live. If I were to create an event around volleyball in their community, it probably wouldn't have much of an impact. It depends on where you live. This is true of sports such as hockey, lacrosse, and even golf. The moral of the story: make sure you know what people in your community care about and what they enjoy so your marketing efforts don't fall flat.

Community Involvement

Most people don't spend enough time developing a strategy. They throw together any old event or campaign and then wonder why it wasn't effective. A good local marketing plan isn't only about you, your company, and your services; it should also involve and benefit the people you are trying to serve. It should support, enhance, or connect the people inside your community. These aren't mutually exclusive either, because you can support and engage your community in a way that can help you build your brand and your business if you're tactful and professional.

What type of local event could you host that would both help the community and raise your own level of awareness? Think of all the local events you've either participated in or seen advertised over the years. This list of ideas can help you get the creative juices flowing:

Consumer Education Events

Why did you first get into this business? What do you love about what you do? For many of us, we do it because we care about educating and consulting with homebuyers. There is no better way to do that than by bringing a group of people together to have a conversation about pitfalls to avoid when buying a home. Hosting consumer education events not only allows you to educate but it will enable you to build a name for yourself in your community. It all goes back to what you care about. It could be first-time homebuyers or VA renovation products but find your cause and target your audience.

Customer Appreciation Events

Research shows that 68 percent of customers change brands because of "perceived indifference."[11] In other words, customers go elsewhere when they feel the person with whom they are doing business doesn't really care if they do business with them or not. Don't be that person.

You may have closed a deal with a customer and then never spoken to that customer again, maybe more times than you'd like to count. Both parties are focused on the future and move on. It's natural. But maintaining a good relationship with past customers is an excellent way to stay relevant in the community and to gain repeat and referral business. Severing ties and moving on after a deal means you're missing out on a golden opportunity. Part of becoming a local legend in your community requires cultivating existing relationships as much as it does creating new relationships.

It doesn't take a tremendous amount of effort to keep those relationships alive. It just requires doing all of these things we've been talking about. You should be connected to your old customers on social media. Like and comment on their posts. Drop them a line on their birthdays or con-

---

11 Voyce, Tracey. "68% of all people leave a business, because of 'perceived indifference' - What are you doing to keep your clients?" *Bloomtools blog*, October 6, 2015. https://www.bloomtools.com/blog/68--of-all-people-leave-a-business--because-of--perceived-indifference----what-are-you-doing-to-keep-your-clients-.

gratulate them on an accomplishment. It takes 10 seconds to shoot them off a personal message if you see something interesting on their feed.

If you want to take things to the next level, consider hosting customer appreciation events. Make them networking events. Invite past customers and encourage them to bring friends who might be interested in your services. Encourage local real estate agents to stop by. Don't be afraid to get creative.

For example, there was a team in Irvine, California, I admired for going above and beyond for their clients by arranging for a taco truck to come to their closing. They sent out mailers and invited people in the community to meet the new homeowners. A couple hundred people showed up because who doesn't love free tacos? It was a great way to celebrate the loan, and it was an excellent way for everyone involved to meet new people. It was all for a good cause, and it was branded strategically.

You don't necessarily have to try this idea. Find something that works for you, your clients, and your community. Housewarmings, block parties, and client appreciation nights can achieve the same thing and help you celebrate with the clients for whom you just closed a loan.

If you like this concept and see the value in maintaining relationships with your previous customers, stick around.

We'll do a deep dive into strategy and execution in later chapters.

Toy Drives

Both toy drives and book drives for kids are great events to host around the holidays. I can't think of a single person who doesn't want to help out kids. Also, you can do it for charity so the people who help out can get a tax deduction. I know teams that do this every year and have been wildly successful at both helping out the community while promoting their business and generating prospects in the process. You'll always want to utilize social media when promoting events, but different events require a different approach and a different strategy. Does your community have any online newsletters or community event calendars? Don't forget your local newspaper as well. They likely have an online calendar and are often looking for stories. They might even feature your event! If so, utilize those resources to make everyone aware of who you are, what you're doing, and how they can contribute to your drive. Set up collection times in a public location that are sponsored by your business. Don't be afraid to make pick-ups and accommodate the people who want to help out.

Community Cleanups

What better way can you give back to your community than by organizing a neighborhood cleanup? You will literally help make your neighborhood a better place to live. Before you get too carried away, go down to city hall to see if the city is planning its own cleanup. If not, ask if you need any permits or licenses to organize one.

Don't try to throw something like this together; first come up with a plan. Pick a specific area, like a beach, park, or field. Identify the number of volunteers you need and outline their particular tasks. For an event like this, you might need supplies. If you ask around, you might be surprised to learn that some hardware stores will provide free donations for community-related tasks. For events that take place out in the community and are for a good cause, it doesn't hurt to take a lot of pictures and post them on social media to spread the word. See if you can get some press in the local newspapers. Don't expect them to give you a full-page press release but it's helpful to build relationships with the local media and have them in your corner when you host future events.

Additionally, you should explore the differences between press releases, actual stories, and advertorials. If you need to learn about these differences, do yourself a quick Google session.

Leverage Existing Events

You don't always have to put together an event from scratch and build the entire thing from the ground up on your own. Think of how many events are already happening in your area. Just go to the main website for your city or town to look for upcoming events. When I was growing up, there was a huge community yard sale every year. Everyone would put all of their junk for sale out on the street and we'd walk around buying up each other's junk. People came in from out of town. It was great!

The point is that if you know an event like that is coming, it gives you time to plan, collaborate, and promote. Old-school websites like Meetup.com are places to find events and people with similar interests in your community. Patch.com is another platform that allows you to see local events and even promote your own. Local newspaper websites and community Facebook groups are also loaded with information. Opportunities are out there; you just have to find them.

Utilize What You Know

I was at the mall recently with my wife and kids. We were getting burgers when I happened to spot this Lincoln car dealership selling cars inside the mall, like Tesla. But that's not what stood out to me. I also noticed they were hosting a rescue dog adoption right there at the dealership. Of course, my kids ran over and jumped on the dogs because that's what kids do. I started talking with the people running the event, and they told me the owner of the dealership really cares about dogs so they had organized a promotional event. I was blown away. What a great idea!

If you care about rescue dogs, you're probably already donating money or volunteering at a local shelter. If so, why not organize your own event, help the community, and spread the word about what you do in the process? You have an opportunity there. You may not be interested in rescue dogs but there is something out there that you are passionate about. You'll just need to figure it out and how you can make it a component of your brand and your business.

Here's another example. I met Brian at a new hire orientation. We had cocktails at the bar and tried to figure out some local marketing plans he could use. After kicking around some ideas, we stopped talking about work and he started telling me what he did in his spare time. Ironically, that's when we figured out how he could improve his business.

Brian was an outstanding runner who also coached high school track. He cared about kids and running. I don't know how we got on the subject of running shoes but it turned out that the kids on his team outgrew at least one pair of running shoes every season. That was the basis for our idea. Instead of all of these kids throwing out their running shoes at the end of the season or having them sit in the back of the closet indefinitely, Brian would ask the kids to bring their old shoes into school so he could collect them.

How many other schools needed running shoes? How many nonprofits needed running shoes? Brian went home, did some research, and came up with a plan to create a shoe drive. He asked parents and kids to donate their slightly used running shoes, or to donate brand new ones, so that he could distribute them to other kids in need. Not only was he able to make a massive impact on the lives of other student-athletes at various schools in his area but he was able to brand himself in the process.

Brian isn't the only person I've watched marry his personal love with his professional passion. Jonathan was a colleague who loved racing custom-built RC cars. When he first told me about it, I had no idea what he was talking about. I had to look it up, and I saw that the type of racing he did looked incredibly fun. He was able to lean into that interest by hosting a quarterly race for kids that was sponsored by the company he worked for.

Do You Have a Third Place?

Ray Oldenburg first wrote about the concept of a third place in his 1989 book, *The Great Good Place*. It's a relatively old book, but I love it and think it's spot-on. Think of a third place like your home away from home and work. For many people, it's a restaurant or a bar but it could also be a church, gym, golf club, coffee shop, community center, nail salon, hairdresser, or barbershop. It's a welcoming space where you can be social and engage with like-minded people. It's a place where you enjoy going. It's not a chore, and usually it's the next best thing to setting up camp in your own living room.

No matter how cool your house is, you need to get away sometimes. Too many people today, particularly in major cities, become isolated and seek comfort inside their own carefully constructed bubbles where they engage with the outside world only through their various devices. It doesn't matter how much you engage online; you will always be disconnected from the community if you don't get out there. Neither Netflix, Instagram, Facebook, nor the evening news can truly fulfill your social needs.

It doesn't help that the more time we spend on our devices or in front of our televisions, the more negative news and outrage we unconsciously ingest. That can cause even the sanest person to think the sky is falling.

Ironically, the more connected you are online, the fewer people you encounter during day-to-day interactions, and the more isolated you can feel while losing empathy for other people. That's why a good third place can have a massive impact on your life and psychology.

Like Cheers, a third place should be void of any social hierarchy so that Mike the stockbroker and Joe the barber can have a conversation about anything regardless of income bracket. It's a place for discussions, not fights. There's no agenda or dress code. It's neutral ground. Think of it like this: Both the French Revolution and the American Civil Rights movements began in salons and barbershops—two of the most important third places in history. Some of the coolest events going on in any area tend to fly under the radar, and people only learn about them through word of mouth, so you have to be plugged into your community. A third place is a great way to be plugged in.

Too many loan consultants today don't have a third place, which means that they are missing out on an opportunity for expression, connection, and growth. For those of you who don't have a third place, your homework assignment is to find one. For those who do, your homework assignment is to utilize that third place. Try to think about how you can engage with your community there. Do people at your third place know that you do loans? If not, they should. Start simply by wearing a branded T-shirt there and then work up to something bigger. It may sound easy but our biggest strength is our ability to build relationships, and if done correctly and authentically, it can be way more impactful for your business than any Super Bowl ad.

If you're one of those who doesn't yet have a third place, here are two ideas to get you thinking.

#1. Do your kids play sports?

One excellent third place so many people overlook is their kids' sporting events. If your kids play sports, sometimes it may seem like your entire weekend is spent around a tournament. You befriend other parents, and in a way, those sporting events become your third place. The next time your kid has a soccer game, try getting there early, setting up a tent with your company logo and handing out food and drinks. You could also bring orange slices and Gatorade for the kids, maybe something different to offer the adults, but be sure to keep it PG because you're at a family-oriented function. This allows you to let people know what you do. You don't have to shove it in people's faces but get to know them a little better and make sure that they know you are the person to turn to if they have a mortgage question.

#2. Let's face it, for most people their third place is a bar.

If you like socializing and sharing the occasional adult beverage with friends, utilize your local watering hole. It's already a very popular third place. And the type of bar that serves as most people's third place probably isn't a chain restaurant, it's usually a local establishment with an owner. You probably even know the owner or the person who runs it. If you don't, that's a problem you can fix. If you go there often, get to know the owner. Once you get in good with the owner, ask if you can host an event. Find out what nights are slow and come up with an arrangement that might help both of you out. I've watched people do this and I've watched it work. You can utilize your local bar or restaurant in many different ways, but don't forget to do it strategically. That's where branding and marketing come in. You want to get the word out in a way so that people know exactly who you are and what you're trying to do.

Follow Up

Throwing a successful event is half the battle. It's an important and crucial piece of the puzzle, but it means nothing if you don't follow up. Whatever the event you're organizing, you want to make sure that you're collecting information. You'll want to ask for contact information from those participating so you can thank them. Following up with personal notes is a great touch. No one who participated was obligated to help so be sure to reward them. Depending on what type of event you're throwing, offer food and drinks. Maybe throw a party if you're doing something out in the community. You could host a raffle and give away prizes.

You'll also want to collect information so you can get your name out there, talk about the services you provide, and attract business. It's essential to do this tastefully because you don't want to rub anyone the wrong way. Don't be pushy or obnoxious. Always ask permission. If somebody isn't interested, drop it. You can't expect to win over everyone. That's not how this works. If you get one or two leads because of an event, that's a win. It's one or two more potential customers than you had before you started.

And remember, just because someone isn't interested in your services right now doesn't mean they won't look you up down the road. If your name is out there, you're known in the local community, and active on social media, potential customers will more likely call you when they need a loan. If you did a good job branding and marketing, you will be the first person who comes to mind and you'll have a good chance of being their first call. That's how this works. It's the advantage of becoming more visible in your community.

Burgers & Benefits

I have to give it up to Bill Gaylord and the Gaylord Hansen Mortgage Team in Nevada for putting together an absolutely brilliant local marketing strategy.

Bill started in San Diego and he built some momentum

behind his local VA homebuying seminar, before moving to Las Vegas, where he tried to piggyback on that success. He got on his social media, did all the press, and promoted the heck out of the event but he couldn't get anybody to show up. Bill wasn't doing anything wrong. He just hadn't been in the area long enough to build up a following and establish his name as a local expert and professional.

Bill didn't complain. He didn't come up with excuses and he didn't give up. If the vets didn't come to him, he would go out and find the vets. He located the local military base and saw that there was a big shopping mall across the street. He put two and two together and assumed that a lot of the military personnel went across the street for lunch so he scoped out the mall food court. He started at the Five Guys restaurant, went up to the manager, and asked, "Sorry to bother you, but do you mind if I ask if any veterans come in here?"

"Yeah, vets are in here all the time. Why?"

"Is it okay if I set up a kiosk in the corner and offer to buy free burgers for any veterans who come in?"

"I don't get it. What's the catch?"

"No catch. In the seven minutes it takes to cook their burgers, I want to explain to them some of the VA home-buying benefits they might not be aware of. I'm passionate about the subject and want to educate vets because many don't know about these benefits. Also, I want to buy them a burger and thank them for their service. If they aren't interested, they aren't obligated to do anything, but I have more information to provide those who can take advantage of these benefits."

It turned out that the manager was a veteran and loved the idea, so the next day Bill came back and set up a kiosk in the corner of Five Guys from 11:00 a.m. to 1:00 p.m. During that two-hour window, 30 vets came in—and 18 of them agreed to sit down and take him up on his offer. He took their order, paid for their burgers, and walked them through the presentation he had prepared about VA home-buying. He then thanked them for their time. By 1:00 p.m., Bill had spent $200 of his own money and walked out of the restaurant with three pre-quals.

Bill cared about educating vets, so when his first efforts came up short, he got creative and found an even better way to connect with his target audience. He stirred up even more business than he would have had his initial idea worked. Bill expanded his original idea and gave it a name: Burgers & Benefits. He now hosts them on back-to-back days so if the vets return to Five Guys with a buddy, they can both get a free burger. Bill used the momentum from the Burgers & Benefits program to host quarterly VA homebuying seminars where he fills the room with up to 40 vets every event.

Thanks a Latte

How many of you go to coffee shops regularly?

I'm sure a lot of you do—it might even be your third place. The next time you pull up a seat in a coffee shop to work, put a sticker on the back of your laptop that says something like, "free lattes for first responders." It could also be for teachers, firefighters, or police consultants. It could be any group that you care about and think might be underserved in your community. The point is that people will see your sign, come over, and say something like, "Hey, I'm a first responder. Why are you handing out lattes?"

You reply, "I just want to say thanks for your service. I also have some unique loan programs that might interest you. You can take this information or give me your email."

You just have to put yourself out there a little bit in your local community to make an impact. You'll be surprised by how many people will engage with you and how easily you can generate interest and influence. Plus, it's more beneficial doing something like this in a coffee shop while you're working than it is sitting locked inside your office looking at your email. You can potentially kill two birds with one stone.

Can you do something like this in your local community and impact the people simply by being an educator and offering them information? Start with what you care about. It's amazing what will happen and what causes you will discover when you focus on what you care about. Dive in. Don't wait for the customers to find you. Go out and get them!

Lean In

Let's say that you've just hosted your first event, you got a handful of people to show up, and it was a success. Now you want to look for ways to capitalize on that success, build on that momentum, and further expand your influence and visibility. You could turn that first event in the local bar into a quarterly happy hour to thank former customers. Invite real estate agents to play a role. Host educational seminars. I've even seen some loan professionals work out a deal with bar owners to get an item on the menu named after them. One guy even arranged to have his face and contact information on the coasters. Yup, coasters. And it worked. People who come into the bar remember that. It takes a special kind of person to want to have their face on a bar coaster, and you may not be that kind of person, but the point is: The sky's the limit. Don't be afraid to get creative. Once you've gotten in good with the owner and have your face on the coasters, maybe even work out an arrangement to send coupons to past customers. It all starts by looking for ways to engage with customers at a cool place and developing a consistent experience.

As with any of this stuff, there is no formula for what to do or how often. Figure out what works best for you and allows you to be consistent and repetitive in your efforts. You have to make sure you do it, but there is also such a thing as "too much" when it comes to local marketing—sometimes less is more. If you're hosting an event at a local bar or restaurant, stick to doing it quarterly or twice a year. Trying to put together something every month might be overkill.

And only do one thing at a time. It doesn't matter if it's an educational seminar, a toy drive, or a quarterly networking event, stick to one at a time. A friend of mine is a mortgage professional in Washington and once a year he hosts a pie-eating contest. That's all he does and it's wildly successful. Every November, he starts marketing and invites people from all over to bring, taste, and buy pies. It's so simple yet so brilliant. You don't have to overcomplicate any of this stuff.

Local marketing efforts can provide a giant boost to your business, but it's important to remember that none of this will solve all of your problems or make you a marketing genius overnight. That just doesn't happen. The point of this chapter is to get you thinking. Some of the ideas I've laid out here might not be a good fit for you or your business. That's to be expected. What I want to do is get the juices flowing. Take some of these concepts and figure out how to adapt them so they do fit your business. Once you start flexing those muscles, you'll get used to using them. Start with something you care about. Leverage your digital tools and social media outlets. Get yourself out there. Impact your community and make a name for yourself. That's how you earn the right to sit at the table with potential customers who need your services.

Just Show Up

A couple of years ago, I ran a contest in our office that I think is just as relevant today as it was back then. The slogan was simple, "Be There!" That's it and it didn't have anything to do with results. Results are good. That's how we get paid, but this contest focused on just being in the game.

We created a leaderboard and gave points for things such as going to open houses, making cold calls to real estate agents, going to broker previews, and sending out mailers, emails, and texts to customers and prospective customers. It was a contest in which we got points, literally, for showing up. At the end of each week, we ranked everyone, and it wasn't a shocker that those who did the best in this contest were the same people who got the most results.

What you may not realize is that showing up is half the game. Just get out in front of people. You don't even have to be good. We all know people who generate a lot of business, even though we may not think they are particularly good at what they do. Tag those people and call them out! I'm kidding. Please don't do that. Instead, take the time to think about how they get their business. Chances are they show up and put themselves out there.

The point of the contest was to encourage people to stop overthinking. Stop looking for the perfect solution, pitch, or flyer because those things don't exist. Just get yourself out into the community and online because that is where the people you need to reach are. Give them a chance to see how amazing you are at what you do. The biggest pro tip in the game is just to show up.

PART IV

THE POWER OF REFERRALS

CHAPTER 7

How to Identify Potential Referral Partners

Here's a test. Before diving into this chapter, I want you to conduct another audit that will help determine your level of visibility. Take a step back, look at the current state of your business, and answer these questions honestly. Before we put together a plan, you have to know what you're starting with.

- How many real estate agents do you work with consistently? Or maybe a better way to phrase this question is—how many real estate agents would say they consistently work with you?

- How many leads are you generating from your referral partners monthly?

- How many deals did you close this year that were directly attributed to referrals from real estate agents and builders with whom you work?

- How much total business are the agents that work with you actually doing in your marketplace?

- How could you capture more of that business?

No judgment here. This isn't meant to make you feel bad; it's meant to show you ways that you can expand your business and become more visible. If your answers to these questions make you realize that there is more that you could be doing, think of this as an opportunity you haven't tapped into yet.

As with anything else we've discussed this far, you don't want to dive in blindly or throw caution to the wind. You want to come up with a plan, and when it comes to finding referral partners, it starts by developing a target list of qualified prospects. Who are the best real estate agents out there? Who are the real estate agents you want to work with?

This requires some tact. Don't simply go after the top one-percenters and call that your list. As you will find when we get further into the process, you might be setting yourself up for failure. Get strategic. Pay special attention to the influencers in the real estate space, even if they don't fit the ideal profile.

For example, I knew a guy back in the day who seemingly didn't do much business at all. He kind of floated around his office and did only a couple of deals a year and we became buddies. It turned out that he was a social connector who could introduce me to those big dogs. Pay attention and spot those people whom you see at every mixer, training session, and board event.

Yes, you'll want to identify the agents whom you plan to prospect, but you also want to identify what those agents care about. When you know what they care about, you know how to help them and provide value, which is the first step when it comes to forming a relationship.

What do agents care about? There is no one-size-fits-all answer but it often depends on their experience:

- Newbies: These are the agents with under two years of experience in the business and with fewer than 10 transactions. Typically, these agents are focused on the process, so you can answer their questions and provide help through simple tools like flyers at open houses. You don't have to meet with these agents one-on-one; you can meet with them in groups.

- Solo Agents: These agents have 25 to 50 units where they are driving 100 percent of the sales. They tend to care about quality, loan experience, saving time, and how you can help them grow. That typically means helping them build a team or add an assistant. If you find a solo agent without an assistant, that person is probably ready to pull their hair out. They're working 70 hours a week or more so the biggest way you can help them out is to save them time.

- Small Real Estate Teams: These agent teams have 50 to 250 closings. It's important to understand their team structure. As a group, they might have the same values as solo agents, but they also care about training, developing, and managing their team. You can help them by comarketing and cosponsoring events. Some of these agents may be looking to hire a transaction coordinator so they can leverage off their buyer showings and spend more time taking listings. They want to get more leads because they are the least profitable agents as a percentage, so anything you can do to help them increase that profit margin is a plus.

- Mega Teams: These are the giants with 250-plus closings. These are the Chris Hellers and the Mark Spains. A lot of them were top-notch businesspeople and CEOs before they got into real estate. Their focus is on lead aggregation and building their team. That's how you can help them.

You have to understand your market, who the best people are in your market, and what they care about because they will all have different needs. Don't forget to talk to your own management. They probably know all of the best agents around. Use all of the information and resources at your disposal when building your prospecting list. Come up with 50 names. Come up with a 100 if there are that many quality agents in your area.

Now that you have your names, it's time to come up with a strategy.

CHAPTER 8

Eight Ways to Grow Your Referral Business

Think of this list like a menu where you can pick and choose the strategies that best suit you. You don't have to do every single one. In fact, some of these strategies might not work for you. The best loan consultants tend to pick two or three and dive in deep because that's where their strengths and resources lie. What are your strengths? Which of these ideas can help you skyrocket your business? Whatever the answers are, double down in those areas. Don't spread yourself too thin, though, by trying to do too many different things.

#1. Digital Marketing and Social Media

As we've emphasized digital marketing and social media throughout this book, it's fitting that it's our number one strategy. And by this point, you should be good at it. Utilize the same strategies that you did to build your network. Remember ICE?

I – Identify the top agents.

C – Connect with them on social media.

E – Engage directly and through digital marketing.

Commenting and liking posts is an easy way to get to know somebody, but it's important to remember that you don't want to be creepy. Think of social media as an online cocktail party. You wouldn't walk into a regular party and start screaming about how you have the best rates. Maybe you would, but you shouldn't, so don't do the same thing on social media. Just be human and think of it like a normal relationship. Take the time to learn about people, engage with them, and find out what's important to them. Find out what you have in common. Connect by talking about something that matters to them. It often comes down to two main areas:

- Important business events: This includes new listings and successful closings.

- Important life events: This includes events such as getting a new dog or having a child graduate.

These are the topics that matter to your referral partners, and if they are already posting about these events on social media, it's perfectly acceptable for you to reach out and engage on those topics. Chime in and congratulate them on accomplishments. Who doesn't like compliments and being congratulated? Be consistent, but don't over engage. Before you know it, you will build an online rapport, but this strategy works best when combining it with other strategies, such as our next one.

#2. Face-to-Face

Let's move from the digital world to your local community. It's much easier to make an impact when meeting someone in person than it is online. Don't forget that your local referral partners are out there in the community. You just have to know where to look so you can get in front of them.

Every strategy you come up with should have a result tied to it. Don't do any of these randomly. For example, my face-to-face strategy was to attend a specific number of open houses between Thursday and Sunday. They weren't just any open houses or broker previews; I targeted the ones involving the top agents on my prospecting list. When I started doing that, I saw one agent four days in a row at four different open houses. Finally, on Sunday he asked, "Are you going to walk in every time I have an open house?"

"Yes," I squeaked out because I was terrified.

Luckily, he laughed and told me, "It took my last loan

consultant two years to earn my business. Keep showing up. I love it."

You want to be proactive but it's also important not to move too fast. Try breaking down your face-to-face strategy into three phases.

Phase One: Get to Know You

When starting out, you're just making your presence known. You aren't selling any products or services yet. Don't start throwing flyers in a real estate agent's face. They don't know who you are and they don't care. Every loan consultant has their boilerplate pitch, but the reality is most real estate agents aren't paying attention if they don't know you.

Focus on introducing yourself and making a connection. You want to appear likable and trustworthy before you try to forge a business relationship. Just because this relationship is being forged in person, it doesn't mean that you can't utilize social media. Connect with them online to learn what they're interested in so you can find the common ground. Ask them how things are going but don't be rude. Be respectful of their time because they're working. Understand who your prospect is as a person, and if all else fails, get them talking about every real estate agent's favorite topic—their sales. One of the best questions you can ask a real estate agent is, "How many deals did you close last year?" Ask about their business. "Tell me about your team. What are you going to do this year? What's the next level for you?"

A common misconception is that real estate agents hate loan consultants but this is only true if consultants give agents a reason to hate them. Of course, there are jerks out there or agents who are just having a bad day. You will come across some people like that and when you do, don't waste your time. Just move on. The reality is that most agents aren't like that. If you put in the time and effort, eventually you will get through to them and make an impression.

You'll know that you're out of phase one when you walk into an open house and the real estate agent knows your name.

Phase Two: Build a Rapport

This is also known as the "offer value phase." By this point, you're already showing up day in and day out so your prospects know who you are. This is when it becomes appropriate to start offering up things of value. Start small by offering to bring financing flyers and bottled water to open houses. Maybe you can help to promote their listings further. Pay special attention to how they respond. You'll immediately know how much your prospect trusts you and where you stand. If you get a hard "no," that means you'll need to work harder to build that rapport. But if they accept your offer, the prospect knows that they will owe you. Even if you get an answer like, "No thanks, I already have a guy who brings water" or "Maybe next week," don't give up. Follow through and prove you're consistent.

Be bold. Put yourself out there. Don't be afraid to send a note to a prospective real estate agent with links to marketing material. You can say something like, "Hey, congrats on your listing. I wanted to go ahead and create some marketing for your listing to help you sell that home. Check out this website. Congrats and good luck!"

It doesn't have to be a game either. Sometimes you can come right out and ask, "We've met a few times. What can I do to add value to your business?"

None of this happens overnight so you'll need to be patient. This phase can go on for a long time before you can get your prospect to bite. But once you do, open up the conversation. "Do you do single property websites? Do you care about search engine optimization (SEO)? Here is our total expert suite. What do you think about this stuff?"

Phase Three: Trust

It's difficult to reach this phase but it's accessible when you put in the time. Just for frame of reference, that agent who told me it took his last person two years to get his business gave it to me in six months. But I put in the work. I never missed an open house. He wanted me to bring cookies, so I did. It became part of my routine.

What was that routine? Well, rain, shine, sick, or healthy, I made sure to hit eight open houses over the weekend. When I returned to the office on Monday, I'd take all the flyers from the open houses, track my activity, send handwritten notes to all the real estate agents, and immediately connect digitally with everyone to keep tabs on what was going on. It started all over again on Wednesday with broker preview days. Friday, I'd check back in with the agents to find out who was working that weekend and where. Through it all, I kept bringing cookies to that open house and then one weekend, that real estate agent called me up and said, "I'm sitting with some customers. Can you pre-qual?" That was it.

You know you're close when real estate agents start asking you finance questions or think of you as a resource. You want to be the loan consultant who real estate agents go to with their questions, no matter how unrealistic the questions may seem. "Hey, can we do a condo loan in this neighborhood?"

Consistency and discipline are the keys to getting into this phase. Some agents are quicker to bring you into this phase than others. That's where the patience comes in, but this phase will truly begin when the potential prospect takes a meeting with you to discuss a partnership. In the meantime, they may let you put some flyers in their open houses, create some single property websites, or bring some waters by a broker preview, but a sit-down business meeting to discuss how to become actual partners in real estate is the goal.

Throughout this entire process, you have to be resourceful. If you aren't, some other agents will be and they'll acquire that business you're pursuing. You'll also want to look out for being caught up in the loan consultant friend zone. Real estate agents will take your flyers and allow you to bring water to open houses but you eventually reach a point where you must ask for business.

#3. Monthly Intentional Contact (MIC)

Once a month, check in with your prospects and try to add value. You can do this through email or snail mail but the point is communication and maintaining contact. It sounds simple and easy but this is too often overlooked or delegated out and that's not good enough.

Let's keep it simple: Come up with 12 different ideas for maintaining contact to send your agents that are intentional, authentic, and creative and that can make an impact. Here are some suggestions:

- An e-flyer about you and your company

- A direct mailer to the office with an "about me" section

- A video message via email or social media

- An open house survival kit

- A fun and silly gimmick mailer like a stress toy in the shape of a house

- Email marketing tools

- A personalized slydial voicemail

  - And if you don't know what that is, give it a Google!

- Share a MortgageCoach Total Cost Analysis (TCA)

- Share a useful application of business tips

- Share your business plan and strategies for the next year

Some people like getting economic news. When meeting with a client, most real estate agents want to be the best-educated agent out there and the local economist of choice. So if you can share information on the local market, special programs, or where rates are going, it makes you look smart and it arms your potential partner with the same knowledge.

If you are going to use snail mail as an MIC strategy, it's important to remember to add a personal touch. If you send 100 identical letters to every agent at a big office, they're just going to throw them away. Instead, try sending your package to the agent's house. Also, sending a package via delivery or that requires a signature will also make an impact. The point is to do something different so you can stand out in a way that your prospects will remember.

Don't forget, real estate agents love to be recognized among their peers. Lean into that. Maybe you can create a monthly award for the top producers in your area. Pull the data. Host a vote. Post it on social media. Drop off actual awards. Have fun with it.

I used to send personal monthly newsletters—not email but paper, sent to the office or home the old-school way, through the mail. But mailing just a standard envelope will not get their attention. Most of the time, people don't want to read mailed newsletters. I learned early that I would have to make it interesting, so I used to send my newsletters out in a cardboard tube because most people will open that out of curiosity alone when they get it in the mail.

I also mailed people small bricks (real bricks) with a note attached that said, "Let's build a foundation together." It didn't stop there. I sent out some fortune cookies with a message inside that read, "Your next loan with me will close successfully." I even sent a little eyeglass screwdriver with a note that read, "Don't get screwed by your lender. Call me." That wouldn't be something I would do today but it was funny at the time.

Next, I went to six different banks and tracked down 100 crisp, brand-new five-dollar bills. I had calculated that if you made $185,000 a year, one dollar was worth a minute of your time. So I sent my prospects a note attached to a new five-dollar bill that read, "Here's five dollars for five minutes of your time to review my propaganda packet." Of course, it didn't win over everyone. Some people sent me the money back. I even had one real estate agent incorrectly accuse me of violating RESPA, but I had so many more people call me up to say that they thought it was hysterical. The stunt worked.

My all-time favorite promotion was when I arranged to have a couple of bobbleheads of myself made so I could send them around to a few different offices. I had them made in China and I ended up looking Persian, which I thought was amazing. The whole point was to draw attention to my brand and let people know what it was I did. Some people thought it was funny and I won them over. Others found the whole thing too cheeky for them. One ancillary benefit of establishing your brand is that you will weed out the people who are not a good fit for you or your business because they will choose not to work with you.

That will save you the headache of having a professional falling out.

Shortly after sending out those bobbleheads, I showed up at an open house held by a real estate agent on my prospecting list. He pulled me aside and said, "Dude, I gotta tell you something."

"What?"

"The bobblehead."

"Yeah, how was that?"

"I don't want you to be mad but your bobblehead is now an award we pass around the office for the 'Bonehead Real Estate Agent of the Month.'"

I wasn't mad. In fact, I was flattered. I became "the bobblehead guy!" How great is that? All of that stuff helped me stand out to the real estate agents I wanted to do business with. I'm not suggesting you try these exact strategies; in fact, I'd probably advise you not to do some of them but do try something and see what sticks.

#4. Leveraging the Other Agent

It surprises me how many loan consultants don't think to do this one. Some of us do it, but not consistently or intentionally, and it should be a part of your strategy. Your ability to prospect and engage the other agent intentionally is crucial to growing your business.

Let me explain. Every time you work on a business, there is the one agent who referred you and then there is the other agent you're working with. That is typically the listing agent but if you work with home buildings, it will likely be the buyer's agent. That's a great way to add value and meet a new agent in the process. It's low-hanging fruit. In a low-inventory market, a lot of the good loan consultants will tell the other agent, "Hey, when you're making an offer, let me know, and I can call the listing agent to help sell your client."

Part of your day-to-day blocking and tackling plan should involve you getting a face-to-face appointment with that other agent. It shouldn't be something that you do when you happen to remember; it should be a goal that you set out to achieve at the beginning of the process.

First, you have to perform well and prove your worth. That other agent has to see that you're professional and good at what you do or they won't want to work with you. Of course, you're going to knock it out of the park on your loan. It's what you do. But even if you don't knock it out of the park, you still have an opportunity. Call the agent and say, "That's not how we normally do it. I've got an appraisal waiver coupon for the next client you send my way because I want to show you how it should work." That goes a long way.

#5. Setting Appointments

What's your appointment strategy?

Most people don't have one. This is also often relegated to an organic occurrence and not a strategic plan. Let's lean into it. To create deeper relationships, we must have business meetings with our referral partners. They can be informal. They can happen over coffee. You don't have to be in a suit and tie and the meetings don't have to take place in a boardroom, but you do want intentional meetings where you talk about your plan to grow your business together.

Do you have a target number of appointments you want to set each month? This should be another blocking and tackling strategy you build into your business plan to develop referral partners. It doesn't really matter what that number is. What's important is that you change the old habit of not having an end goal in mind.

This strategy really has two parts, and people often forget the second part, which involves how you can be effective in these meetings. Let's back up even further. When should you call an agent to set a face-to-face meeting? I did this wrong for a long time. I was overzealous and didn't think of the bigger picture, but I learned that it's crucial for you not to even set meetings until you can offer value.

Here's an idea: Find an agent who has a listing that's been on the market for a while. Let's say it's a non-warrantable condo subdivision. Call that agent up and say something like, "Hey, I noticed you have this listing. I'd love to get together and show you some financing options that might help you sell it a little faster."

Look closely at the agents you're prospecting. Which one took a listing on a dump? How can you help them out? "Hey, I'd love to come in and talk about how a reno loan could save this property."

Or how about something like, "I noticed you have a property that can allow customers to buy it with zero percent down. I have several down-payment assistance programs that can help you put it in front of more buyers and get it off the market sooner."

If you hit real estate agents with specific tools like that, you're doing what most loan consultants aren't doing: You're noticing a specific problem and offering a specific solution. That's so much better than cold-calling or coming up with some generic pitch about all the great things your company does. Agents will love the value you're bringing. That can be game-changing and it will get you that appointment.

#6. Invites and Events

Sending guest invites gives you more reasons to call up your agents. Inviting them to events in your area is an excellent strategy because every month there is a ton of stuff going on. No matter where you live, I guarantee that dozens of events are already happening in your area. Look at what's happening with your local board. Check the Facebook groups and simply invite people to things you see happening. "Hey, did you hear about this training that's happening by your office? You should come with me to it."

You might be hosting a reno or a first-time homebuyer seminar. Great, invite your prospects. The most successful loan consultants host fun events, like wine tastings. And just because you're doing something fun, it doesn't mean that it has to cost a ton of money. You can organize a wine tasting and charge people $20. That's reasonable and it takes some of the financial burden off you.

One loan consultant I know rents a bus every month and invites 50 real estate agents to join him as they ride around to see 10 different property listings. That's followed by a networking lunch. Another loan consultant I know is friends with the owner of an exotic car dealership. They've worked out a mutually beneficial arrangement. He had 40 agents show up at this event where they could look at and drive all these crazy exotic cars and it didn't cost him anything. The owner loved the idea because the loan consultant brought him 40 potential new customers. Sometimes it really comes down to providing people access to cool things.

#7. Ask an Agent

Sometimes the simplest way to get ahead is to ask. It's so simple that people forget it's even an option. And if you're looking to meet the best agents, who knows them better than other agents? So why not ask those people you have a relationship with to refer you to other great agents?

As with every other strategy on this list, it has to be done intentionally and consistently. Make it a point to do this quarterly. Put a to-do reminder in your calendar if you have to. Just like you don't want to call up an agent cold or without reason, you'll want to have a script or pitch ready.

A strategy like this can be helpful because sometimes those top 1-percent agents you want as referral partners don't go to open houses—they often have their teammates or juniors there instead. It can be challenging to get in front of those top agents for a face-to-face conversation so it helps to lean on your network.

Don't limit your thinking. Get creative. Golf has four-somes for a reason. Ask your buddy to invite his agent friend to come out and play golf with you. You don't play golf? Make it tennis. Don't play either? Set up drinks. The point is, it doesn't really matter what you do—it's all about being social and hanging out. At the end of the day, people are more likely to do business with you because they like you, not because they think you're the best loan consultant around.

You'll be shocked by what can happen if you only ask. Don't miss out on any opportunities because you didn't try.

#8. For Sale by Owners

I didn't think of this one on my own but once someone told me how this could work, I nearly fell out of my chair because it's such a good idea. Some even call it the fastest source of business out there.

To start, go to Zillow and click the button that says "for sale by owner" to see all of these types of listings in your area. These are the sellers who don't want to hire real estate agents because they don't want to pay the commission but they would love to talk to a loan consultant. You can save them a bunch of time. Here's a simple way to approach these buyers, "I know you're getting a lot of calls from buyers now and it's difficult to tell who is qualified and who is not. One service I can provide, at no cost to you, is that I'll talk to any buyer who shows interest in your home and needs financing. I'll make sure that they are all qualified and ready to go. If they do move forward, we'll help you do the transaction."

Even if they don't move forward, it's a great way to grow your business and meet new buyers. You can also discover leads that you can then pass along to real estate agents. "Hey, I work with a 'for sale by owner' who is sending me buyers to prequalify them. In fact, I just have a buyer who qualified but the house ended up not being for them. Would you mind working with them and showing them some other property?"

Also, if the homeowner is moving somewhere else, chances are that person might need a loan as well. In the event the owner struggles to sell their house, you can always refer them to a great real estate agent. These are all just some of the benefits of being a talented local loan consultant who is plugged into the community.

None of this stuff works by itself. You don't just put these strategies in motion and then sit back and relax. It's like exercising or eating healthy: You need a plan and you need to execute. It doesn't matter which strategies you choose but pick the ones you think will work best for you and make them a part of your schedule. Don't just say that you're going to do it; make sure that you follow through because consistency is what will lead to results.

Don't overcomplicate it either. Here's a simple idea: Try to meet two new agents a day. That's 10 a week and 40 a month. Do that for six, 12, or 18 months. Think of how big your network will grow. You'll soon have more business than you'll know what to do with.

PART V

LEAD
MANAGEMENT

CHAPTER 9

Bucketing Your Leads

Congratulations! You are well on your way to becoming visible, which has translated to referrals and leads. You've gotten what you wanted, but that's only half the battle. Now what?

Back in my glory days, we expected real estate agents to incubate and lead manage our customers for us. Even as recently as 10 years ago, loan consultants would say to real estate agents, "Call me when they're in escrow." Lead management wasn't a skill set that we had to develop in retail because we relegated it to our referral partners while we operated near the end of the sales funnel. Oh man, how things have changed.

The level of integration we're doing now with our referral partners when it comes to lead management is insane. You'll want to get comfortable doing this because the ability to manage and convert leads has evolved into a crucial skill of the modern retail lender. This might be one of the most important chapters, but I have to admit that it might also be one of the most boring—and that's probably one of the reasons why so many loan consultants are bad at this stuff.

Today, leads come in from everywhere, not just real estate agents. They come in fast and furious so you need a system to manage all of them. The best tool you have is your Customer Relationship Management system (CRM). However, no CRM will solve all of your problems. A tool can only be effective if you use it correctly. If you're using a screwdriver like a hammer, good luck with whatever it is you're trying to build. A lot of us aren't comfortable in the CRM and haven't mastered it, but now it's time to cut through the noise and flex that muscle so you can become a legendary lead manager. You won't need to learn any big secret. It all comes down to being organized and having a system.

How Do You Manage Your Leads?

We all have different strengths and weaknesses so some of you may be stronger and further along in this area than others. For those of you just starting out, I know lead management strategies can go really deep really fast. That can be overwhelming, but I promise we will stay in the safe, shallow waters so that you can understand the basics while playing catch up.

Again, this is the audit portion of the chapter. Sick of it as you may be, it's still an essential part of the process so roll up your sleeves and put in a little effort. Be honest with yourself when answering these questions so you can first identify and then improve upon your weaknesses to grow your business.

- How do you describe your current lead management systems or activities?

- How do you track leads and contacts today?

- Do you have a system that you use for tasks and follow-up management?

  - If so, what is it?

- How do you describe your origination tactics to take a lead and to convert that lead into an opportunity?

- How do you identify your current sources of leads?

  - Real estate agents
  - Landing pages
  - Purchase leads provided by your company
  - Home builders
  - Digital marketing campaigns
  - Local marketing campaigns
  - Zillow
  - Past customers

- Open houses
- Lead pool

Most of you will answer these questions by saying your system is an Excel spreadsheet or a sticky note. If you're a sticky note person, that's fine. I used to do lead management with a stack of real estate agent business cards. We must have a system, but chances are if you aren't utilizing your CRM, that system is inefficient, outdated, and costing you business. That stops today. Let's learn how to get those potential customers back into your sales cycle.

What a Lead Is Not

What's the difference between a lead, a contact, and a transaction?

- **Leads:** A lead is a short-term opportunity for you to track and eventually convert into a contact and a transaction.

- **Contacts:** A contact can be a current or past customer, a business partner, real estate agent, builder, or a teammate.

- **Transactions:** A transaction is directly linked to a lead or contact.

The leads discussed in this chapter are the short-term

opportunities you want to turn into buyers. These are the folks you meet at open houses, passing by at an airport, or as potential customers your referral partners send to you.

Categorizing Your Leads

Not every lead is created equal. Different leads are further along in the process and different stages require different approaches, or workflows, to convert those leads. Those workflows become your system, and they help you manage and contact those leads efficiently and consistently no matter how much volume you're dealing with.

Before we get carried away, let's first define our terms and list the different types of leads you'll be working with so we're all on the same page.

When starting the process, most leads can be bucketed into one of two categories:

- **Cold Leads:** These are the potential customers you found without a formal referral or previous introduction. These include leads you get from Zillow, BoomTown, new home registration lists, open house lists, etc. You're starting at the bottom with these leads, which means you will have to work a little harder.

- **Warm Leads:** These are typically referrals, so

unlike with your cold leads, these potential customers have been told about you or your business. As a result, they are likely to respond to you quickly. These referrals can be through real estate agents, homebuilders, past clients, friends, family, etc.

The entire purpose behind managing a lead is to move those potential customers toward an objective, which is the next step of the process or into the next bucket. If you're starting with a warm or cold lead, the ideal next step is to convert them into an active lead. What's an active lead?

- **Active Lead:** These are the customers you have contacted and verified that they are shopping for a new home. They have not yet become preapproved or prequalified. They may or may not have decided to work with you yet but you know they are actively looking and there is a chance of your earning their business.

- **Nonactive Lead:** Not all leads will pan out; in fact, most of them won't but you won't know if you don't try. These leads in the nonactive bucket could be cold or warm leads you've made contact with but learned they are not proceeding with a loan. However, that's not the end of it. There are a lot of reasons why a customer might decide not to move forward. It doesn't mean that you can't eventually convert that lead, which is why you want to bucket these leads into two subcategories.

- **Contact:** These are the customers for which, even though they are not currently shopping, things might change down the road so you want to maintain contact and keep these potential customers in your ecosystem.

- **Noncontact:** These leads are hopeless and not worth your time. They are the people you don't want to stay in touch with, for a variety of possible reasons, that I will leave to you to define.

As we've established, not all leads are created equal, and the further along in the process a lead is, the less work you will have to do but that also comes with more competition for the lead's business. That is why you need to be on your A game when trying to woo the leads in these next two buckets.

- **Prequalified:** These leads are the real deal. These are your Glengarry leads. This is an excellent bucket to be in because these customers have already gone through the prequalification process and are actively looking to buy a home. The goal here is to move these customers into the very exclusive next bucket.

- **Preapproved:** These customers are fully underwritten and have been credit and asset approved. They are good to go, and now it's your job to convince them to work with you. Just remember that you aren't the only one approaching them.

Life is messy and not everybody can be easily defined or put into a box. The same is true about leads. You will have all kinds of leads that might fall in between some of these buckets or others that come with their own extenuating circumstances. Here are some examples:

- **Past Client:** These customers have finished the loan process and either withdrew or were declined. They were not successful in funding and it's likely they could be repositioned as either nonactive or into our next bucket.

- **Nurture:** These customers were actively interested in buying a home but through the application process, or due to everyday life events, they needed more time before they were ready to proceed. Those reasons can be anything from having poor credit to merely needing to save money.

CHAPTER 10

Warming Up the Cold Leads

The definitions for each bucket are important because leads at different stages in the process require different strategies. Those strategies are what we call workflows, and a workflow has a straightforward objective—take something from A and convert it into B. So whether you have a cold or a warm lead, you'll want to convert that to an active lead. Workflows are intentional and designed to move the customers further along in the process.

Even with the help of workflows, the responsibility is still on you to put in the work and do the actual converting. No magic tool will suddenly do all of this for you—you have to utilize the resources at your disposal and put a system in place. This is easier said than done, and I know because I was never the best at this. I had to learn, like I do with most things, the hard way. Like all of you, I was busy, so sometimes I would call and pre-qual a customer but then forget to follow up. Maybe my sticky note fell off my computer and then two weeks later, I suddenly remembered the Johnsons. I called them and learned they had bought a house without me. I was crushed.

That's a familiar story, and I know that I'm not the only person this has happened to. Given the sheer number of leads we're bombarded with, it's much more common today, and more and more of these leads are likely to slip away or fall through the cracks if you don't have a workflow.

Managing Cold and Warm Leads

Very few people truly like cold leads. You know I'm not wrong but you still have to keep track of them and you'll need a tool that can handle high volume. So when a lead comes in from a real estate agent, social media, or loanDepot's Digital Purchase Lead Program (melloLeads), the very first thing you want to do is put it into your CRM. Methods can vary depending on where you work and the tools you use. But you want to get in this habit because failing to put leads into a lead management system is the easiest, and most common, way for things to go awry. Start there.

What comes second is the contact. This is where you have to be proactive. Make it easier on yourself, and if possible, call this lead right away. This is especially true of warm leads. If you call those warm leads right away, it will lead to a much higher contact rate, which means you can move them into the active bucket much quicker. Get in the habit of doing the same thing every single time with every single lead so it becomes second nature.

When I talk about workflows, I'm talking about a systematic plan of how and when you will contact each of these leads. You also want to know what you plan to say or send. None of this should be on a whim. Here is a process I use that involves making five different attempts to contact that lead.

Attempt #1: Even though I've just covered this first step, it's worth repeating: Warm or cold, call your lead right away! Have a script prepared for voicemail that talks about who you are and what you do. "Hey, I'm Alec Hanson from loanDepot. I got your information through my real estate agent partner [or through Zillow]. I'm in the local market and would love to talk to you about the financing options we provide." It's that simple.

If I know the sales price, I'll tell them something like, "We have tons of options for low down payment or aggressive financing. I think you might be in the market for something like that. I'm going to send you a follow-up text right now with some more information."

I would then immediately create a MortgageCoach Total Cost Analysis and text it to that lead with the sales price and the loan amount with a simple message that reads, "Here's the information I was talking about."

That's my one-two punch. You can do whatever you want. Maybe you want to send a video to follow up. There is no right or wrong answer. Figure out what works best for you but it must be intentional and systematic.

If you do make contact, you don't even need to worry about the rest of this workflow because the first step is complete. You then move that lead to the next bucket and the next workflow to proceed accordingly. If you don't make contact...

Attempt #2: You won't want to make this attempt the very next day. It might be a week or a month later, depending on the situation. No matter what your time frame, you can simply follow up with a call or an email. Many of you have great personal commercials or videos that explain why you're in the mortgage business and why you like helping customers. Maybe send that in your follow-up email. If you've put in the legwork creating content and building your brand, you should have a library to choose from.

Attempt #3: If you still don't hear back, follow up again. Maybe you send them some self-drive options. Have fun with it. "Hey, I see that you're a first-time homebuyer. I just created a series on this topic and hosted a seminar. You can check out the videos on my Facebook page."

That way, you follow up and you can potentially engage with them on social media. If they aren't first-time home-buyers, maybe they are veterans or could be interested in renovation loans. Find that need and look for ways you can provide value.

Don't forget that everything we're discussing in this book is connected. Mix and match all the tools you have in your belt. Getting to know your leads better through social media and making a connection there is another great way to convert them. Find them on LinkedIn or Facebook and make a request.

The same is true for your campaigns. See if you can get your leads interested in any of your current campaigns. Send out invites but don't wait around for the campaign to convert them. Do that in addition to working these steps, not in place of these steps.

Attempt #4: Some loan consultants quit after the third try but I like to follow up again a fourth time. If I haven't heard back, I will send a simple takeaway script by texting something like, "I believe you have everything you need, but if you have any questions or want to discuss further, please call me."

Attempt #5: Why not try one more time? This is actually my favorite step. It's a simple goodbye text that reads, "Did you get everything you need for your loan?" That's it, but you wouldn't believe how many times that gets a response. It's amazing! By this point, some of them might just want to get rid of you, but if they don't have everything they need, or if they are confused, they will most likely reach out.

Neither you nor anyone can be expected to remember all of these steps for all of your leads, which is why utilizing your CRM is so important. Get organized. Set yourself reminders and block out a certain amount of time each day or week for lead management. It takes systematic organization to make sure you get done what you need to get done without any opportunities falling through the cracks.

Managing Active Leads

The next bucket I want to break down is the one with those active shoppers. These are the people you know are out there and looking for homes. You may or may not be the one they decide to work with but they are the people you should be stoked to have conversations with. The cold/warm workflow is designed to get people into this bucket. They are further along in the process and they are familiar with you so they require a different workflow. Now that you have an active lead, what should your first step be?

Step #1: If I knew somebody was shopping for a home, I would call that person every Friday. That's crucial. In fact, it's Lead Management 101. Set a reminder because you won't be the only person calling those active leads every week. You can send them a text but remember that everyone is marketing to them so you need to stand out and stay top of mind. Make sure your content is engaging. You should also make sure to tell them that, while they're out looking for homes that weekend, you'll be working and available if they have any questions. I guarantee you that the best lead converters do that every single week.

Step #2: If you haven't done it already, connect with them on social media so you can try to build a relationship. Comment on things they care about. Throw them a like here and there. Don't be rigid and all about business. This is important, and it's something a lot of loan consultants forget when they have their eyes on the prize, but don't just pound your leads with marketing material. That's overwhelming and it could rub them the wrong way. You want to be helpful and provide value but you also want to be a human being. Remember that people are more likely to do business with you because they like you rather than because they think you're the best loan consultant around.

Step #3: When you think about it, all of these steps are different variations of step one. It's about staying in contact and being consistent. Find creative new ways to keep in touch and provide value. You want to be repetitive in your communication but original in your approach. Let's put it this way: What do you do with all those generic marketing emails you get? Do you really read all of them or do you just hit delete without even opening them? Be bold and break the mold.

Don't forget, you can also break down active leads into two secondary buckets:

- Prequalified
- Preapproved

The truth is that you should handle the people who are preapproved and prequalified differently than those who aren't and the strategies are slightly different as well. You want to approach those who are not yet approved or qualified with the same level of intensity and excitement but (and it should go without saying) you want to push to get them preapproved. Engage them. Get them into your ecosystem. Direct them to your website. Walk them through the process and give them what they need. That's how you can provide value. The sooner they are approved, the sooner they can begin shopping.

Managing Nonactive Leads

Obviously, this workflow is designed for those nonactive leads that you want to stay in contact with. You will get some people who will flat-out tell you, "I have no idea why I clicked that button and am talking to you right now." Feel free to delete those leads from your CRM. This bucket requires more of a laid-back approach that occurs over a longer period, but here are some ideas you can mix and match:

- For those customers who put off actively looking for a home for whatever reason, you can start by using your campaigns as a tool. Put them on a drip campaign so they will get something from you regularly.

- Add these nonactive customers to the invite list for any seminars and local marketing events that you might be hosting.

- Make it a point to text, call, or contact these customers every 45 to 60 days to check in. "Hey, thinking about our last convo. Are you still in the same place, or are you ready to start looking?" That will make an impact, and it might even get them moving.

It may sound simple but the truth is the only way you can stay on top of this is with a plan or a workflow. Will you remember all of this on your own? How many sticky notes can you fit around your computer? Sixty days is two months. Will you remember to follow up with all of those nonactive leads two months after you last contacted them? Those customers will probably be the furthest thing from your mind and you theirs, which is why it's so important to give yourself reminders and make sure that you follow through.

Improvise and Go with the Flow

Again, "No two customers are the same." There are different subcategories for various types of lead buckets and you'll want to accommodate their particular needs. For example:

- Let's say a client in your nurture lead bucket delayed their search because of credit issues. Try emailing them helpful articles or resources on repairing their credit. Given the situation, adjust your timeline to follow up accordingly.

- For many purchase leads, you're looking at a six-month conversation, which means you need to develop a six-month workflow that will take them from contact to active to shopping. Some of these customers don't have real estate agents. So if you're doing a great job with local marketing and digital marketing, you're probably getting there before the agent.

- For in-the-market alerts (ITMA), we at loanDepot let our consultants know if their customer has their credit pulled somewhere out in the wild. What is your workflow for this situation? Stay consistent and create a workflow similar to your cold lead workflow to keep that customer.

Real Estate Agent Lead Tracker

How great is it that the real estate agents we work with refer customers to us? Wouldn't it be even better if we could go back to those real estate agents with a list of those leads and a detailed report of how we're managing them?

Some of the best teams in the world do this with their referral partners. This is the future, and we have a system at loanDepot that tracks your leads for you and will give you back this report every week. The report provides important details like how much they prequalified for, in which state they live if they have their documents, and if they are preapproved. You can do this right there in your CRM where you have all of this information, which is why you have to make sure you are utilizing all of these tools at your disposal.

You will look good to all your referral partners when you can physically show them the progress you've made with each referral. It shows you're on top of your game, and they will be more likely to refer customers to you in the future because you've shown that you know what you're doing.

What's Your Action Plan?

The good news is that if you are out there building your brand, working with referral partners, and pumping out digital and local marketing, it will work and it will generate a lot of leads! The downside (and this is a good problem to have) is that when you're dealing with so many leads from so many different sources, you can quickly find yourself in the weeds and completely overwhelmed. That's why you want to keep things simple. Don't overthink this. If you find yourself overwhelmed by this, or worried that you are the type of person who might get overwhelmed, start by creating three buckets:

1. Warm/Cold Leads
2. Active Leads
3. Nonactive/Staying in Touch

Create a detailed workflow for each bucket. You can utilize the plans that we've laid out in the chapter or you can modify them to fit your needs better. Keep in mind you need to be realistic. Don't set outrageous goals that you won't be able to follow through with or achieve. There are countless ways to do this, but the keyword is that you must "do" it, so make sure you find what works for you. Choose your own adventure but remember these key points.

- Come up with a three-to-five-day attack plan that taps into the resources and content you have at your disposal.

- Set yourself reminders to make sure you follow up with every single lead.

- Set aside time in your weekly or daily schedule to follow up with everything related to lead management. Maybe you tackle it all in one day. Perhaps, you break it up and tackle different buckets on different days.

- Don't forget to connect with your leads on social media. Engage and connect over important life events.

- Invite them to events that you're attending or hosting in the area.

- Be consistent. This doesn't mean be overbearing or annoying but do remain in contact so you're on the top of their mind. Don't be afraid to let them know you're working while they're out looking for a home.

- Provide value. Don't just send them any old content or make small talk when you reach out. Instead, try to help them with a specific need or problem.

All of this is a numbers game. You aren't going to convert every lead. You just won't, and often that has nothing to do with you. However, if you don't follow up and you let things fall through the cracks, you won't convert any leads. But if you have 200 to 300 people in your cold and warm buckets and you work the plan to make sure you maintain contact, you will slowly build momentum. You will move some of those leads into the next bucket and so on. It's like you're rolling a snowball down the hill and watching it get bigger and bigger until soon it becomes an avalanche.

As with most everything else, in the end, it will come down to you. My message for you is to own your workflows. It's human nature to want to sit back and have someone or something else do all the work or solve the problems for us but that's just not going to happen. You have to execute your own contact strategy and craft an experience for your leads to see results. You have the opportunity to master lead management. Set out to dominate your space and be the best in the industry. You are supposed to be hunters so go out and hunt!

PART VI

CONSULTATION
AND QUOTING

CHAPTER 11

Are Your Conversions Better Than Most?

You can do everything right. You can brand yourself as a genius and market your business like nobody else in town. You can rake in countless referrals from all the top real estate agents and contacts. And that's great, but none of it matters if you can't convert those leads. At the end of the day, it all comes down to *conversion*, which is why I think this part of the book is one of the most important.

Given the way the industry is today, we are all under tremendous pressure to be great and deliver an even greater experience. Consumers want it all—they want the best price, service, and execution. To make things even more difficult for you, many companies are out there disparaging the loan consultant. There is a competitor, who will remain nameless, who is running advertisements blatantly saying that loan consultants are ripping people off!

It's a whole new mortgage world out there, and it's the reason why the local loan consultants have become invisible. Information can so easily be obtained online. This is anecdotal evidence, but my experience shows me that nearly 80 percent of customers coming in through a referral already have a quote or a pre-qual before they even reach out to the loan consultant. This drastic change in customer behavior demands an equally radical shift in the way we provide our consultative services and deliver an interest rate quote to the customer.

How can we break the cycle? What's the trick? For starters, instead of asking yourself how you can be successful, try asking yourself how you can be useful. You need to prove your worth and your value to the customer and that often comes down to providing the correct information so they can make the right choice for themselves. Understand your craft, be an expert in your field, and know your numbers but don't forget about the human element. The longer you can engage with the customer, appease their fears, and answer their questions, the stronger the relationship. Can you see the pattern that's developing?

And it isn't just me saying this. I've spent time with the best and brightest in the industry to gather information and learn how they go about consulting and quoting. No matter how we slice it, our business has become a conversion game and conversion has a lot of interesting parts to it.

Self-Audit

This is really important for those of you who are new to the mortgage business, but also for you old dogs, because I know so many of you out there are quoting off instinct or relying on a process you've learned over time. It's you I want to challenge in this chapter to see that there might be a better way to go about quoting a customer. But first, see where you stand by asking yourself the following questions:

- What steps do you take before quoting a customer?

- How do you describe what your ideal consultation and quoting process would look like?

- Are you using any tools, like MortgageCoach, for consultation and quoting?

- How do you handle common objections to that process and adjust accordingly?

- What's your conversion success rate, and are you happy with it?

The Power of a Process

For those of you who answer these questions and suddenly feel like you've been getting commoditized, there is a good chance you aren't following a plan and don't have a process. You might also be diving into the rate too soon or letting the customer drive the conversation. All are common mistakes that lead to lackluster conversion.

Think about it this way: If you were a real estate agent and you came to me, a loan consultant, with some referrals, you would want to know what I plan to do with those referrals. You would want to know how I'm going to crush it because, as a real estate agent, it's important to you that I convert your lead. You want me to give the customer, and you, confidence.

This doesn't mean, however, that every customer will be willing to follow your process or your plan right away. In fact, I can promise you that not every customer will follow the plan. That's just how it works so it's important that you are able to pivot.

I will lay out a plan for you and discuss some common objections you are bound to hear sooner or later. As with the other tips and pieces of advice in this book, none of this is written in stone. This process won't work for everyone so think of it as a starting point. Everyone brings something different to the table and that's how you differentiate yourself from the competition. That starts with being a human. Too many loan consultants essentially become glorified order takers. I'm going to talk a lot about the technology and tools you need to be utilizing but they should enhance what you do, not replace it.

Everything You Do Is Public

You may already know this but if you don't, it's worth repeating: Everything. You. Do. In. Sales. For. Your. Customers. Is. Public. Think about that for a second. It doesn't matter if it's your sales pitch or your emails, everything you do will be reviewed by other people. If you send someone a quote, guess what? They are forwarding that to someone else— friend, family member, accountant, or whoever. I saw one customer who posted an exchange with their mortgage professional on Reddit. (If you don't know what Reddit is, it's probably for the best, because it's the pathway to the dark web.)

It's for this reason that I love technologies like MortgageCoach, BombBomb, and Vidyard, which provide transparency and allow you to talk customers through what you're showing them. If you aren't the one walking them through the process, they are asking for help elsewhere, like on Reddit.

Think of this a different way. The fact that everything you do is public is awesome because now you have a much bigger reach within the community. It's also a great reminder to put a little more thought and care into what you're telling and sending a customer. How differently do you handle your communication when you know other people are listening in? Think about that when you're drafting emails. Ask yourself, "What if this were posted online?"

Put a sticky note on your computer to remind yourself that everything you say and type will go public, and I guarantee that it will help you consistently bring your A-game to every interaction.

CHAPTER 12

Hopes and Dreams Become Reality

You've followed all the steps in the previous part perfectly, you've taken my advice, and you were rewarded with a lead from your referral source. All of that digital marketing, branding, and referral legwork paid off. Hallelujah! Now what do you do? Of course, you can't ignore that every customer is different. They won't all go down the path you want to lead them but if you don't drift too far from the spine of this strategy, you will out-convert your competition. I like to think of this as the optimal conversion path.

Step #1: Initial Contact

Don't forget what you learned earlier in this book. Take that lead and put it in your CRM; don't put it in Excel or revert back to the sticky note system. Once you put the lead into your CRM, contact that lead immediately. "Speed to the lead" is everything and even five minutes is too long to wait. There is no higher priority than a hot lead. If an agent gives a customer three referrals and you're the last to call, you will likely lose that lead and they will go with someone else. So unless you're in a consultation with a client, excuse yourself to call a lead right away. Leave a brief message so there is no stress and then use the follow-up strategy previously discussed.

Step #2: The Hopes and Dreams Call

You won't always get to speak to the lead the very first time you call. Sometimes you have to be persistent and track them down, but when you do finally get a chance to speak, that is when you conduct what I have dubbed the "hopes and dreams call." This important call is your first interaction with the customer so you should spend some time dissecting your options.

Although the first thing many of you will want to do is take the application right away, that's precisely what you don't want to do.

If you're ever stuck, you can refer to this list of questions and action items when trying to get that critical information.

- What purchase price range are you looking in?

- How much is your down payment?

- Source of down payment?

- Payment comfort?

- What is the horizon of you living in the home?

- Explain the digital tools available.

- Confirm whether the borrower is a veteran.

- Confirm "plans for home" (explore reno option if applicable).

- End call with a request to gather the client's information. Take an application.

- "We can do this right now; it takes 15–20 minutes over the phone."

- "We can schedule a time that better fits your schedule."

- "I can send you a link to take the application at your leisure."

- It is never good to send out a link cold.
  Deliver options.

This is not a consultation and it's not all about business. This call is all about building rapport. Remember that you do this every day; the customers don't. They want to be led, so here are some tips and tricks that will allow you to acquire more information while learning a little bit more about your customers and what makes them tick:

- One simple way to get the conversation started is to pump up the real estate agent who referred the customer. Ask how they met. Listen to what they say. Those stories might give you insight into what they're looking for in addition to some of their concerns. It's always helpful to tie the referral source back into the conversation and the referral source will absolutely love it!

- Take the time to know your customer in a personal way. What are their kids' names? What are their hobbies? If you find out birthdays and anniversaries, you can put all of that information into the CRM, even with a reminder to pop up on that day so you can send them a personalized message. You want to interact with your customers on a personal level because they don't necessarily care about what matters to you, they care about what matters to them.

- This call should have nothing to do with rate, conversion, or down payment. If all the customer wants to talk about is rate, you can say something like, "Let's put that aside for just one minute. I know rate is super important, but first, can I ask you a few questions to make sure that we're a good fit?" I've never had anyone say no to that.

- That last part is essential because you need to make sure that you're a good fit for each other. We have all had customers we've hated working with so you want to be on the same page and figuring that out should be priority number one during this call. You might realize you're speaking with someone who is looking to buy an eight-unit building complex, and if you don't do that type of thing, you aren't a good fit so you can refer them to someone who is.

- Take control at the beginning of the conversation and then listen to what the customer has to say. You don't want to start talking about a 30-year fix if they plan to move in four years. Try to understand the customer's wants and fears. What makes this difficult is that not every customer will know their wants and fears right away because they don't understand the process yet. Many are overwhelmed and confused so you might have to read between the lines.

- Alleviate those concerns and fears by catering to their needs and providing value. Think back to your campaigns. Is the customer a veteran? Maybe a first-time homebuyer? Has the customer considered reno? The reality is that when the customer goes out to shop, they might have neighborhoods and markets they like, but the homes they find in that area might not be ideal so reno can be a good option. Providing expert advice is a crucial step that allows you to set yourself apart from a Google search by proving yourself to be a valuable and knowledgeable resource.

Let's take a step back and talk about the bigger picture and how customers tend to have false assumptions. If the customer doesn't bring up any concerns, you can bring up these common false assumptions both as a way to get them thinking and to build trust:

- Customer believes their credit score, or FICO score, is too low.
- Customer believes their student loans make them ineligible to buy a home.
- Customer believes the home they can afford requires too much work.
- Customer believes they don't have enough money for a down payment.

If this call goes well and you feel that you're a good fit, you can talk about next steps and getting them an application. Be sure to let them know you will review their information and that the most important part of the process is the consultation you'll set up shortly.

Step #3: Review All the Client Information

This is the behind-the-scenes stuff. Before you set an appointment and get face-to-face, push the button and run the digital validation tools. You want to provide the customer with a tremendous streamlined experience so don't be afraid to ask for more information if you need it. But don't randomly ask for a laundry list of documents that you might not need. The days of sending an email and asking for a W-2 and two years of tax returns are long gone. It doesn't work like that anymore. If you put in the leg work, you will know what specific documents they need and that makes you look so much better than the competitor who is asking for that laundry list. You do that and you will win all day long. You'll want to go into the consultation prepared and having done your homework. Here are some of the items you'll want to complete ahead of time.

- Custom customer roadmap
- Custom needs list, if applicable
- Pre-built and personalized loan options
- MortgageCoach
- Transaction plan and calendar

Step #4: Set a Face-to-Face Consultation

This is what you've been waiting for. You've gotten the customer preapproved so it's time to bring them in. The goal is to show them you are the expert. Make sure they have all the information they need. Once you start talking about their options, they will have many questions. You'll need to educate them on what matters most to them, whether it is the interest rate, payment, cash to close, cost over time, etc. Walk them through their options and give them a choice. That's what this consultation is for.

You may be saying, "We're in a digital age. I don't need to meet with the client face-to-face anymore." Sure, there will be times when you can't set a face-to-face. But a face-to-face appointment helps to build a stronger relationship and leads to the highest level of conversion.

I also want to challenge the assumption that people don't want to meet face-to-face. Many people assume that millennials live life online, pushing buttons and coming to them through digital memes, so they don't want to meet in person. However, I've been shocked by the number of millennials who actually do want to meet. It doesn't matter your age; a mortgage is a big deal. You're about to get into the biggest debt of your life. People respect that, even millennials. They still want to look you in the eye and know they can trust you.

The face-to-face consultation can get complicated so I want to break it down into a few categories. Here are some things to consider:

A) *When the customer first arrives at your office, what do they experience?*

I always ask this question because it's important but often overlooked. Does the customer walk in and see a welcome sign with their name on it or do they have to track down someone in the back and explain what they are doing there? Some loan consultants have snacks ready, some even have their own food and drink menu. Think about the feeling you get when you walk into Starbucks. It doesn't matter what store or what city you're in because they are all the same. That's intentional. What are you doing for your customers that has the same type of intentionality? You have complete control over the atmosphere you create. Not only will that make an impression on the customer but it will get back to your referral source.

B) *Show them your transaction plan.*

You do this every day. Your customers don't, so they don't know what a roadmap looks like. They don't know the milestones, what needs to be done to close on time, or what happens when they are in contract. Showing your customers a transaction plan can lower their level of stress because it allows them to see in advance how the process will unfold. Have this filled out before the meeting so you can tell them specifics like, "If you give me a 28-day escrow, here's how I'd handle it."

C) Include a calendar to complement the transaction plan.

Walk them through the steps and give them assurance with statements like, "This is how we back in the dates to protect you and make sure the appraisal gets done on time. I'm not only going to update you but I will update every agent every single week with our plan of execution." This also lowers the customer's stress level by letting them know what's coming next. You want to send this calendar out at the beginning of the transaction to both the listing agent and the buying agent. Incoming calls slow you down so you want to get out in front of that by letting everyone involved know you have a plan and you're in control. It's a game-changer that gives the customer confidence. It proves you can close and execute and all before you've even talked about rate. If you can't close, rate doesn't matter, so you'll have to have this conversation.

D) Eventually, yes, you do have to talk about rate.

You've gathered all of the information you need, now it's time to use all the tools at your disposal to deliver the customer a curated quote that lays out all of their options. Educate the customer on their options to help them make the best decision for themselves. I believe MortgageCoach is the best tool available to help the customer understand their options and take them where they want to go. But don't take my word for it, go check them out on YouTube and make your own decision. Not many loan consultants use this tool so this is another way to differentiate yourself. You'll want to create the total cost analysis before the customer comes in and have it on the screen, ready to discuss. Show them their rate, their payment, and their cash to close. This is complex stuff. I've talked to financial advisors who don't understand this, so the customers will have questions, which is good because the goal of this consultation is to alleviate concerns and meet their needs. You don't want to just deliver the rate and disappear. MortgageCoach is a way you can do all of this. In the long run, it will save you a ton of time.

The customer had a curated experience upon entering your office, was greeted, and felt welcomed. You talked about the process, how it works, and went through various scenarios and options to let them decide what's best for them. You answered their questions, alleviated their fears, and showed them your unique value proposition. They know what's coming. They might have an idea where they want to go. They like the buy-down. They like the different options. Some might have already found their dream home, some might be ready to go shopping, and others might be six months away. What do you do now? Do you sit back and wait for them to make a decision? Of course not.

Step #5: Follow Up

Don't forget everything you learned in the lead management section. Now that the customer has reached the prequalified stage, you want to follow up at least once a week, along with every other lead in your prequalified bucket. The last thing you want to do is put in all of this work only to forget to follow up and have the customer go elsewhere. It will happen. Trust me.

You have so many tools at your disposal so try to get clever. You can always call or text but how about sending a video follow-up? It's memorable, stands out, and can be a good use of your time while simultaneously reminding the client of your value. What's most important is that you contact clients before they ask to be called, and always keep them updated about where they are in the process and possible next steps.

Step #6: The Preapproval Letter

There is a lot of confusion and misinformation about this letter in our industry today. After a great consultation where we get the customer preapproved, the first thing they are going to want is their letter so they can go shopping. The problem is that we can't just whip out a letter. Well, we can but it won't do the customer any good. Nobody likes to hear that but it's not how it works.

Let me explain. There are so many preapproved letters floating around that are absolute garbage because they never went through an underwriter. The loan consultant just typed "approved." You don't want to do this. You want to put your customer in the best possible position with the buyer, and you do that by taking the time to send out a customized prequalification letter. When the customer does find their dream home, you want to create a letter that is specific to that home. When the letter is ready, call the listing agent, introduce yourself, and let them know that your customer is making an offer on that home. That will separate both you and your customer from the pack.

You want to create a reputation for yourself so that preapproval letters from you have power. When you have a letter that says you met with the customer face-to-face, validated their information, have fully underwritten approval, and everything else is done, that carries more weight than a generic letter from some bank. It shows you do things differently than the guy online or the competition down the street. It will also help get your customer's deal into escrow so you become known as a leader and an expert in your local market. If you're going to become visible once again, you want your reputation to be positive and to be known as the best.

CHAPTER 13

Handling Modern Customer Objections

Nothing is foolproof, and you will meet customers who don't want to be led down the preferred path or who have objections. It's unavoidable because customers have concerns. The trick is to become familiar with the most common concerns and have a response ready to go when those concerns arise. However, don't be a robot. You don't want to read off a literal script or deliver the same information the same way every time. You'll want to encapsulate the message but find a way to deliver it uniquely and authentically to each customer.

The objections we face today are different than what they were a few years ago, but here is a list of the most common issues industry leaders face when attempting to follow the preferred path to convert.

#1. The customer doesn't want a face-to-face meeting.

Yes, a face-to-face meeting is the best way to build a rapport and convert but we've all been there and it isn't always possible. That's not the end of the world. The next best step would be to try and set up a live phone conversation. With platforms like Zoom and Skype, you have many ways to replicate the face-to-face format and communicate live. MortgageCoach even has similar technology built-in so you can speak to each other live. Sure, you can always do a regular old phone call but ideally you want to bring another element into the equation beyond audio because it creates a more personalized interaction. How many loan consultants are taking this extra step? Honestly, not enough.

A straightforward way to encourage a face-to-face with a reluctant customer is to email them a MortgageCoach TCA. When they open the link and see all of the information, they could very quickly realize there is more to this than they assumed and they'll want to set up a more personalized meeting to go over the information. Maybe they don't respond, but it might be just what you need to open that door and help you convert that lead.

#2. The customer doesn't want credit pulled.

Simply inform the customer that they have 45 days to have their credit reviewed by multiple mortgage lenders. Their overall approval and quote is determined by their credit score. If a lender were to quote the customer without performing a credit score, it could be misleading. Your goal as a loan professional is to be as accurate as possible. That will benefit the customer and also allow you to provide all the programs the client might be eligible for. If the customer doesn't believe you, reference the article put out by the CFPB that addresses this, or better yet, send them the link: https://www.consumerfinance.gov/ask-cfpb/what-exactly-happens-when-a-mortgage-lender-checks-my-credit-en-2005/.

#3. *The customer wants a quote before providing the necessary documentation.*

As you know, many different factors go into a rate, so the less information you have, the less accurate the quote. We can always provide quotes, but that's all they are—quotes. Wouldn't it be better to provide a real solution instead of just a quote?

#4. *The customer says they are only interested in getting the lowest rate possible.*

This is a big one because so many customers don't realize the complexity of what we do nor do they understand that the lowest rate might not be their best option. Most lenders can offer customers the same rate but the difference may be the cost associated with that rate.

#5. The customer communicates that "cash to close" is too expensive.

Ask which costs are too much and what are they basing that on. There are ways to cover some of the costs. You could adjust the rate to add rebate. Before quoting the rate, advise how much the cost was reduced. Then compare the cash to close with the new payment and explain the rate and how rebate works.

#6. The customer comes preapproved from another lender.

That's great! This allows the customer to compare lenders and ensure they get the best offer or program available.

#7. My real estate agent is also my lender.

Lenders and real estate agents are two separate pieces to a mortgage transaction. You should recommend the customer work with a direct lender (like yourself) since you specialize in providing the best financing possible for your clients.

#8. The customer found a cheaper rate online.

This may be true, but the customer has to understand that the rates found on internet sites are effectively advertisements that they must call and inquire about. Once you go through the process with an online lender, there will most likely be some additional costs or requirements needed to meet the advertised rate.

#9. A competitor offers a lower interest rate or fees.

Commend the customer for doing their research and ask when they received the loan estimate from the other lender. If they didn't receive it, ask why not. If they did, walk them through how a loan estimate is constructed and recommend they confirm how long the rate will be protected.

Putting It All Together

Go back over the preferred path to figure out your individual strengths and weaknesses. Is there a step you're skipping or maybe a weak link in the chain where you tend to lose customers or fail to get leads to the next level? Perhaps, you're doing the hopes and dreams call but aren't setting any face-to-face meetings. If so, rethink your strategy and your approach to that call.

Engage with the customers. You don't want to be just an order taker and you don't want to just fire off application links. Build a rapport and demonstrate your value by eliminating their fears and concerns. Show them they have options. Be intentional about the experience you provide the customers. You are an expert in your field and in your market. Follow up and stay in touch.

You want to be the one who drives the conversation and the direction of this transaction. For example, if you get a customer who only wants to talk about rates, have the courage to say something like, "You and I might not be a good fit." It isn't easy to say something like that, but it shows you are confident and believe in your system. In the end, people don't want to be sold, but they do want to be led down the path that is the most comfortable for them.

PART VII

MORTGAGE CX

CHAPTER 14

Creating an Unforgettable Customer Experience

What does CX mean? To me, CX stands for one of the most critical aspects of our business: The mortgage customer experience. The responsibility for that experience falls on your shoulders because, whether you like it or not, you are the architect of that experience.

The bar is very high because today we're all spoiled by the Amazons and the Ubers of the world. We live in a world of convenience and instant gratification where we can get so many different things with a click of a button. However, when it comes to the mortgage experience, it's often like we're going back to the Stone Age. You can change that. It starts by creating an intentional process with transparency and clear expectations for the customer.

What makes you more effective, and more importantly, what makes you visible to the public is if you do this every single time. Don't forget that you are a customer too! Think about the experiences you've had. What do you gravitate toward and why? What experiences delight you as a customer? Now think about how that translates to the mortgage industry and what you do. Put yourself in your customer's shoes and try to think about what it feels like to be them—a person who doesn't do this every single day and could easily find themselves overwhelmed. Think about what they want and why. You don't have to think very long to realize we're behind when it comes to creating an enjoyable experience. You know there's a problem; you just don't know how to fix it.

You may or may not like Starbucks but no matter where you go, even in another country, Starbucks gives you the same experience as soon as you walk into one of their stores. You see the same counter, the same apron on the baristas, and they all write names on the cups. It's dialed in.

Are you dialed in? What is it you're doing now? Can you deliver a piece of paper or a video that explains every single step of your process? I bet you can talk customers through the steps, answer their questions, build rapport, and use certain tools, but I also bet that you don't have a system and you aren't taking the time to be as thorough as necessary upfront.

Where Do You Start?

Before you dive into a solution, figure out your starting point by performing an assessment of the current mortgage experience you take the customer through.

- How do you control communication? Is it regular? Is it automated?
- Who is updated when? What are your deliverables?
- Is there a specific mortgage journey they follow?

Throughout this book, you've learned the importance of having a plan, but it's not the plan alone that makes for a great customer experience—it's also how you communicate that plan.

When I say communicate, I don't mean your preferred way of communication; I mean communicating the way that the customer wants to communicate. Do they prefer phone calls, texts, or emails? How often do they want to be updated? That's important to know, as well. Believe it or not, some customers might not want to hear from you all the time. I know, it's difficult to believe but if certain customers prefer only weekly updates by email, that's what you do unless there is an urgent matter you need to bring to their attention.

We all fall into a transactional pattern. We do a loan and then another loan and then another loan and another loan, etc. We get so used to the process that we forget our customers don't do this all the time and they can easily get confused. It's your job to provide clarity and set them up for success by just telling them the truth, not what they want to hear. That's why they're coming to you in the first place.

Transparency also involves:

- Prompt follow-up.
- Delivering items on time.
- Acknowledging sent and received items.
- Providing accurate numbers and documents.
- Explaining how we validate documentation.

Start by explaining to your customers how the process will work from start to finish—that means from application to closing. Keep everyone involved in the process, including your referral partners, updated about the active plan. Then everyone knows, without having to ask, what's happening and in what stage of the process the loan is. If you're having trouble getting started, we've outlined it for you and included a sample worksheet that you can fill out and distribute to each member of your team.

YOUR TRANSACTION PLAN   *loanDepot*

CLIENT INFORMATION

Client Name	John Homeowner
Property Address	123 Dream Street, DreamTown CA 92929
Loan Number	1234567890

CONTACTS

	Name	Email	Phone
Loan Consultant	Alec Hanson	ahanson@loandepot.com	949-500-8062
Production Assistant	Johnny JohnJohn	J.John@loandepot.com	949-500-8063
Buying Agent	Sally Realtor	Srealtor@realestate1.com	949-555-7777
Listing Agent	Kevin Realtor	Krealtor@ldorealestate.com	949-625-8547
Escrow	The Best Escrow	Karen@thebestescrow.com	800-625-8100
Processor	Samantha SamSam	SSam@loandepot.com	949-444-3333
Branch Manager	Alec's Boss	ABoss@loandepot.com	949-111-1111

If you feel you are not getting the best possible service, please contact us.

Bypassed

PROCESS

	Stage	Confirmed Date
☑	PROCESSOR ASSIGNED	10/24/2019
☐	APPRAISAL ORDERED	
☐	APPRAISAL RECEIVED	
☑	SENT TO UNDERWRITING	11/4/2019
☑	CONDITIONALLY APPROVED	11/7/2019
☐	CLOSING DISCLOSURE SENT	
☐	CLIENT CONDITIONS SATISFIED	
☐	CLOSING DOCUMENTS SENT	
☑	EXPECTED COE	1/10/2020

This transaction plan is intended as a tool to keep you informed of current loan status. However, it is not to take the place of personal communication. If at any time you have questions or concerns regarding this transaction or any other currently in process, please feel free to call one of our team members listed above.

If you're ever feeling a lack of motivation to develop or follow through on a plan, remember that the customer is still being shopped every step of the way. You don't want to run the risk that your competitor is communicating more clearly to your customer and promising a better overall experience. Now that you're motivated, read on.

The Optimal Path

None of this is required. There is no one right way to do any of this. All of you are different. As loan consultants, you have various strengths and weaknesses, and everyone brings something different to the table. The path I'm going to lay out is an attempt to start the conversation. It's to get you thinking about the steps you can personally take to curate this process for your customers. Intentionality is crucial. I've talked to countless loan consultants about their own processes, and here are the steps I feel are necessary.

Step #1: The Disclosure Process

How are you setting expectations with your customer? If you're doing this organically, try to spend more time on this step. Communicate with your customer to get on the same page. Make sure they don't have unanswered questions. So many loan consultants tell their clients something like, "You'll be getting disclosures in the mail." Sure, that's okay and it's an excellent first step, but you want to go the extra mile and say something like, "Not only will you be mailed disclosures but I can talk you through them in person if you want to come down." Don't assume what your customers do and do not know. Also, don't assume that the customer will tell you what they do and do not know. That's why you have to ask and be proactive.

Pro Tip: Leverage Personalized Video Tutorials

The process can be monotonous. We find ourselves doing the same thing for our customers over and over again. We also hear the same questions from the customers over and over again. We often think, *Oh, my God! I've done this a million times!*

If you find yourself in that situation, try something different. Spice it up. For example, instead of fielding the same question for every customer, you can create a video tutorial. Record a bunch of videos on these questions and steps to keep in your video library so you can send them out to customers ahead of time. This way, they don't have to come to you with questions. In the long run, it saves you time and makes you proactive.

So instead of just sending the customer an email to inform them that disclosures are coming, you can send a video that says something like, "You're going to get disclosures. Here's what these are. Let me explain it to you." Even if the customer already knows what disclosures are, they can easily skip your video; but if they don't, that video could be a welcome surprise. They may have had questions but were afraid to ask. That happens. This is what it means to curate the experience for your customers.

The ancillary benefit of creating videos is that those videos can be shared. When you wow your customer, they are more likely to forward your videos to real estate agents and friends. "Look at what happened! This loan consultant is amazing!" That's as powerful an endorsement as you can get.

Step #2: Completing Your File

The next steps happen behind the scenes as you prepare the customer's file for the initial underwrite, but that doesn't mean problems can't arise that negatively impact the overall customer experience.

Now your processor will be calling your customer. It's standard they make a welcome call and follow their own script. You know this, but does your customer know this? If they don't, it's your opportunity to jump in and make them aware. Not only that, but you also want to sync up with the processor to make sure that you are both giving the customer a succinct and cohesive message. If this sounds like it should be simple blocking and tackling, that's because it is, but so few loan consultants do this.

Once again, put yourself in the shoes of your customer. How does it feel when you get a call from someone you didn't know would be calling? What runs through your head? *Who is this person? Is something wrong?* It's no different for your customers. It's easy to go into panic mode and this leads to a horrible customer experience. You're also putting your processor in an awkward position. Avoid all of these unnecessary problems by prepping everyone involved and getting on the same page with your customer so they know exactly what to expect.

Step #3: The Appraisal

Why does your customer need an appraisal? Will they ask that question? Do they know what it even is? Time and time again, I've seen loan consultants skip this step. Simply going to your customer and saying, "We're going to order an appraisal and here's why..." can clear up a lot of confusion and maybe even alleviate some of your customer's concerns. You can simply run down a list of the following factors that the appraiser considers during the process:

1. The sales prices of similar recently sold properties in the same area

2. The average time on the market in the area

3. Local sales price trends

4. The balance of buyers and sellers

5. The home's overall condition and grade of construction

6. Number of bedrooms and bathrooms compared to the neighborhood norm

7. Amenities like fireplaces, decks, landscaping, bonus rooms, and garages

8. Home improvements made since the date of purchase

9. The lot size compared to other homes in the neighborhood

10. Neighborhood zoning restrictions

11. A home's uniqueness (unique is not always a good thing)

Don't stop there. It's important to be transparent about the *entire* process. Tell the customer that when you get the appraisal back, it still requires a review and often an underwrite before being released. A lot of loan consultants out there don't want to tell the customer when the appraisal comes in because they know it has to be viewed by the underwriter. I get it. You don't want to get the customer excited only to find out that the outcome isn't good. Get that out of your head, though, because it doesn't matter. Your customers demand transparency. And if you're holding on to information, you are not transparent, which means that you aren't delivering the type of experience the customer expects. Think about it. We don't want to see our Uber driver get lost, but if they do, we want to know when things go wrong. We don't want to be in the dark. So even when things aren't perfect, it gives the customer comfort to know you are on top of things.

The explanation of an appraisal can be one of those

videos you've already filmed about the process, waiting in your library, ready to send out to your customers when they reach this step. And since the appraisal can turn out several different ways, do you have a process for each potential appraisal result?

- Appraisal at value
- Appraisal under value
- Appraisal over value
- Appraisal subject to

"What can I do if the home appraisal comes in low?"

If you have heard that question before, be prepared with a response and a plan of attack. Read the report thoroughly for any errors, like an incorrect number of bedrooms, bathrooms, or square footage. Double-check the comparable properties to make sure they indeed are comparable to the property your customer is looking to buy. If you cannot find any glaring errors in the home appraisal report, you may appeal your appraisal or pay for a new one.

What about refinancing? Are you getting movement? How are you communicating with your refinancing customer about what to do with their appraisal? They will have an appraiser come to their house. Are they ready for that? Do they know what to do? What can they say? Can they share comps? All of these are great potential questions that you can use to educate the customer. Think about it like this: the more information that you provide upfront, the fewer questions and phone calls you will have to field later.

Step #4: Your Initial Approval

You've just approved someone for a loan; what do you do now?

There may be conditions but don't forget that this is important. It's easy for us to forget just how big of a deal this is for our customers and to congratulate them like we should. Some loan consultants send funny texts and gifs. You should have a process so that every time someone gets approved, you do something to let them know you're excited for them. If you're short on ideas, keep reading because a laundry list in the final chapter can help you choose how to wow your customers.

You also need a plan, or an off-ramp, if you have issues and something goes wrong. What do you do and how do you communicate that? Things will go wrong, and your natural instinct may be to withhold those problems from the customer until you come up with a solution. I can respect that, but if the customer is expecting an answer within 24 hours and it takes four days to come up with a solution, you're being disingenuous by withholding information. You're failing the customer. You want to get in the habit of calling every situation out for what it is.

Pro Tip: Request a Customer Testimonial

What better time to request a testimonial than after the customer has been approved? You don't have to wait until closing to ask for a review. I love those loan consultants who are proactive enough to ask customers to post a review on their Yelp, Zillow, or Facebook business page. Think about the psyche of the customer after this initial approval. Chances are they will write a great review. And the likelihood of them shopping you, or leaving you, after writing a review like that is slim. They aren't going to suddenly dump you for an online lender after writing a positive review. When they do write that review, get it out there because it will only increase your conversion and help your business.

Step #5: Your Closing Disclosure

Does the customer have any clue what a CD is?

We have a tendency to use a lot of jargon but don't always take the time to explain it to the customer. This big document they will get can be confusing so take them through the process. Film a CD explanation video that says something like, "You can call me with any questions, but first let me walk you through what you're about to receive..." Tell them what it is, what information it will contain, and why it's important.

Step #6: The Final Sign-Off

This step sounds boring but is actually very important. If you're following the steps and adhering to the process, everyone involved in the transaction should know the loan is in underwriting. However, that's not the only potential issue. I know a few too many loan consultants who drift into the grey area when it comes to the ethics around this step. Maybe they tell the customer that it hasn't come back from underwriting, when in reality it hasn't been to underwriting yet because they're still waiting on documents. Those people should leave the industry. Even if it's your fault the loan isn't back from underwriting, you need to be transparent with the customer about why it's not back. Chances are good that the truth will come out eventually. Don't blame other people. That's a mistake. Own it.

Step #7: Final Approval

Initial approval is cool. You can send a video or a gift, and that's awesome, but with final approval, it's time to blow it up. An email is nice but I would suggest sending a personal video message. Be excited! Celebrate this milestone and let the customer know you're passionate about closing their deal.

Step #8: Closing Expectations

How can you not love this step? The loan is approved! You're all good but closing and funding could be miles apart. Some of you in new construction know that even once you get approval, it might be six months before you close. The lesson here is not to take your foot off the gas. Your customers have high expectations and they are getting information from all different sources, not just you. You have to be overly intentional, as with the other steps.

You can use this Before Closing Checklist to educate them on the closing and funding process:

- Determine who will be conducting your closing, where to be, and when.

- Ask the person conducting your closing what to expect at closing (the process varies by state).
  - What items do you need to bring with you?

- Request your closing documents three days in advance of closing:
  - Closing Disclosure.
  - Promissory Note Mortgage/Security Instrument/Deed of Trust Deed (a document that transfers property ownership).

- Schedule time in advance of your closing to carefully review *all* documents.

- Compare your Closing Disclosure to your most recent Loan Estimate.
  - Are the loan type, interest rate, and monthly payment terms the same?
  - Do you have an escrow account, and how does it work?

- Arrange your payment for the amount due at closing (prepare cashier's check or wire).

During this step, it's good to break out of the restrictive role of being merely a mortgage professional and prove you're more than just a financial advisor. Help the customer understand the human side of the process they are about to go through. For example, is the customer prepared to change their address? Have they done what they need to do with the DMV? The list is endless, so this is where you can step up your game because in doing so, you become much more of their experience.

Step #9: Loan Documents Out for Signature

Have you ever had a notary blow up a deal? Maybe the notary spoke to the customer in a weird way and caused the customer to freak out. This has happened to me before so I'm a little sensitive to it, but this is a problem that can be avoided.

It's so easy to forget what you can control during this process. Remember, you are the master of ceremonies so you can make sure that the notary is on board. Maybe you didn't pick the title and escrow company so you're working with an attorney or notary you haven't worked with before. When you don't know how a notary operates or communicates, you can inadvertently create some confusion for the customer. Has the notary done a hybrid e-closing before? You will want to get out in front of questions like this before the notary speaks with the customer.

If ever in doubt, here's another checklist that you can refer to:

- Bring the following with you to closing:
    - Cashier's check or proof of wire transfer
    - Your Closing Disclosure (compare to final documents once more)
    - A trusted advisor, lawyer, or friend
    - Your coborrower or the person who is cosigning the loan (if any)
    - Your checkbook (in case there are any last-minute changes)
    - Your driver's license or ID

- Get answers to these questions at your closing:
  - How will my property taxes and homeowner's insurance be paid? Is it included in my monthly payment or do I pay on my own?
  - Where do I send my monthly payments? How do I pay homeowners' association dues?

I think it's absolutely epic when loan consultants personally attend closings. You're connecting with the customer at one of the most stressful times of their lives, and you're also proving your worth by doing something no digital loan consultant could ever replicate. Well done! However, this is not always possible. If that's the case, don't do nothing; don't miss an opportunity to wow your customer. Remember, the key to everything we discuss in this book is consistency and the customer experience is no different. How can you make the loan signing special and memorable?

Step #10: Your Loan Funding and Recording

This is it, the final step of the process where we fund the mortgage and the customer takes ownership of their new home. But your work isn't done yet. You want to make sure you run through the finish line and break the tape; don't stop short and walk across. Consider going over these additional items with your customer at the very end:

- Save your closing packet in a secure place exactly as you received it.

- Change your address (bank accounts, credit cards, ID, insurance, US Postal Service).

- Revise your budget and plan for future expenses.

- Review your homeowner's insurance.
  - Does it cover floods? Earthquakes? Other disasters?

- Pay attention to any changes in your monthly payment. (Your payment could go up or down depending on changes to taxes, mortgage insurance, or homeowner's insurance.)

You don't think of what was discussed here as going above and beyond. All of these steps are the baseline fundamental expectations of your customers. If you've executed the steps as discussed and you have videos going out that explain the process, you're doing your job. You're a customer as well, so you know people have come to expect exceptional service, transparency, and accurate information. That's what you want to deliver.

As soon as you find yourself winging it or being reactive, you're doing it wrong. If a customer is calling you with questions, you've already blown it. You have to stay two steps ahead of them. Anticipate their questions and needs. Keep them from shopping and being overwhelmed by providing them all the information possible. And don't be afraid to wow your customer by doing the unexpected. How do you do that? You anticipate their needs and problems and then prove your value by providing solutions.

Here's one example, and for those of you who liked the idea of getting your own bar coasters, you will love this one. When you need to make a big move, you can never have enough moving boxes. Imagine how cool it would be if you could not only provide moving boxes to your customers pre-move-in but if those boxes had your name and logo on them? I'm dead serious. It's cardboard. It doesn't cost that much and you can have a lot of fun with this. Just make sure that the customer hasn't already purchased them on their own.

Here's my challenge for you: Go create your plan! Look at the experience you're providing your customer now and ask yourself if you think it's good enough. Customers are waiting for the magic knight to ride in and utilize technology to do your job for you. If they don't know why they need you, prove your worth. If you put yourself out there and challenge yourself, you can seize this opportunity to become an amazing customer service expert.

CHAPTER 15

Why Mortgage Going Digital Matters

If you have a customer sitting across from you asking what your technology can do for them, what are the highlights you would communicate to that customer?

The world has gone digital and the mortgage world is slowly catching up. Digital tools are evolving faster than we can learn how to use those tools. The foundation of everything we do is moving to a data-first model. In order words, a ton of your personal financial information is available online either in the cloud or protected inside your bank's digital platform. As the mortgage industry continues to evolve, we are going to a place where that data can be connected into our systems to verify employment, income, assets, you name it. When that happens, applying for a mortgage will look at lot less like gathering piles of paperwork and a lot more like simply pushing buttons online.

We must help our customers understand that the paper process involved in getting a mortgage is antiquated and will only slow down the process. I know that is easier said than done, especially today when there are so many concerns about privacy. However, customers who have their income and assets validated digitally through leveraging our technology platform not only speed up the process but they also reduce their cost. What better experience can you provide for the customer than that?

What Do Digital Documentation Tools Do?

Before you can educate the customer, you first need to become a master of these tools so you can walk them through the process and make them feel safe and secure when going data first:

- **Income:** If you can digitally document a customer's income, you get a two-day savings against the normal time it takes to close a loan.

- **Employment:** If you are able to validate employment on top of that, that's another two days, which makes a total of four days saved in the mortgage process so far.

- **Assets:** This is a seven-day savings. That's huge! You will save seven days if you validate your assets digitally. People get nervous about this and are reluctant to put their passwords and logins into the system but you are in a secure system. They can pick their own financial institution, put in their own credentials, and pick the accounts they wish to share with you. Based on their choices, the data comes back to you through the customer.

- **Appraisal:** If you can get a property appraisal waiver, this is a 12-day pickup. Right now, if you check for a waiver with only one agency, either Freddie Mac or Fannie Mae, you get a 15-percent pickup in purchase or 35 percent in a refinance transaction. But if you check both through a Dual-AUS enhanced system, it adds an extra 5 percent on purchase to 20 percent total and a possible 5- to 10-percent pickup on refinance. In other words, it pays to check both agencies for a property appraisal waiver.

So what does this all translate to? For those customers who fit in that perfect sweet spot, you can close a loan in eight days. Eight days! Basically, you're giving the customer full approval on the second day. That is the power of leveraging digital tools. Unfortunately, not every mortgage company has put in the investment to leverage these and some don't have them available at all.

PART VIII

BUILDING RELATIONSHIPS FOR LIFE

CHAPTER 16

Your Job Isn't Over Yet

You made it! The final section. How exciting is this? Congratulations for making it this far. It's been quite a journey, and hopefully, you are well on your way to improving your businesses, strategies, and mindsets. I don't doubt that you're good at this stuff, but like the title of the chapter suggests, you are not done. In reality, it's just starting.

Check out the stats below. I think they would be even more telling today:

- It costs five times as much to attract a customer than to keep an existing one.[12]

- Increasing customer retention by 5 percent increases profits by between 25 and 95 percent.[13]

- The probability of selling to an existing customer

---

12 Saleh, Khalid. "Customer Acquisition Vs. Retention Costs—Statistics and Trends," *Invesp blog*, accessed January 17, 2020.

13 Amanda Stillwagon, "Did You Know: A 5% Increase in Retention Increases Profits by Up to 95%," *Small Business Trends*, updated October 2, 2014, https://smallbiztrends.com/2014/09/increase-in-customer-retention-increases-profits.html.

is 60–70 percent, while selling to a new prospect is 5–20 percent.[14]

As you can see, your previous customers are your biggest referral opportunity. You are dropping the ball if you don't leverage that connection in an authentic human way.

I'm not suggesting you do this—I'm telling you that you *need* to do this. The game has changed. We've reached a tipping point. Those days of being strictly transactional are long gone. Our customers demand that we become relational. If we don't, we will lose and slowly become irrelevant.

It won't be easy. It's not hard to explain this idea but it is hard to accomplish it. Today, transitioning a transactional relationship into a real relationship takes tremendous effort after closing. Generic monthly newsletters and email blasts aren't going to cut it. Sure, you can put them on a drip campaign but how much success will that generate? Today, you need extreme intentionality to deepen that customer connection with a customer who may not need your services again for five to seven years, if at all.

However, you have a tremendous advantage. Let's be honest. You know more about your previous customer than

---

14 Patrick Hull, "Don't Get Lazy About Your Client Relationships," *Forbes*, December 6, 2013, https://www.forbes.com/sites/patrickhull/2013/12/06/tools-for-entrepreneurs-to-retain-clients/#67e759982443.

most of their family and friends do. You have almost every piece of information about them that has ever existed. You know about their finances and have gone through their credit history. How many times has a customer come clean to you and said something like, "Yeah, that's the bank account I don't tell my wife about." You know what I mean. Sometimes it feels like we're doing the job of a therapist. I don't have to tell you this but mortgages are hard! They're hard for us, and they are even more difficult for your customers, but you've led them through this grueling experience so they trust you.

Start by thinking about how you operate as a customer. Think about the restaurants and businesses where you've had a good experience. What made you go back? What made you want to refer friends? I know someone who absolutely loves her favorite coffee shop. Ninety percent of the baristas know her by name, they know her drinks, and what she likes. She loves all the natural light in the space and the fact that she always bumps into people she knows. Those experiences complement the actual product, the coffee. They enhance it.

What kinds of things like this can you apply to enhance your business? Before we get to those questions and come up with some potential solutions, we have to start back at the beginning.

What's Your Visibility Level?

Whenever I run a new hire orientation, I ask everyone how many customers they've lost touch with or forgotten about over the years. How many times have you lost a previous customer's contact information? I've lost touch with hundreds of customers before realizing that I was missing out on a significant opportunity.

So many of us don't have an intentional plan. Before we go any further, take the time to assess where you're starting from so you know what you're missing and where you're falling short. How visible are you to your previous customers? This one is easy. It's just one question. As usual, be honest and vulnerable: what activities are you currently practicing in order to build client relationships that last post-closing?

Big Important Events

Before you make a sample plan, do some brainstorming about some big events or milestones that are important to the customer. It goes back to paying attention to what matters to your customer more than what matters to you. If you want to earn a seat at the table, so to speak, and be considered a trusted advisor and influencer, then you'll need to pay attention to what matters to your customers and use that as the jumping-off point for your engagement.

Customers care mostly about themselves. It's funda-mental. Everyone is different, but here are some universal, no-brainer, big important events to get the wheels turning:

- Customer birthdays
- Their children's birthdays
- Graduations
- Wedding anniversaries
- Sports teams
- Restaurants
- Hobbies
- Pets
- Community events
- Local schools
- Your own customer appreciation events
- Move-in anniversary date
- A new job

You should try to connect over something personal because you know how much you dislike getting generic emails and getting spammed and you wouldn't want to do that to your customers. If you are doing something like this, pivot. Do what you would want if you were the customer. If you were a sports nut, imagine how much better it would be to talk sports with your loan consultant (especially if you root for the same team) than it is to get a generic flyer. (For me, it was Marvel Comics, but you'll find most customers are into less nerdy things.)

So how do you know what your customers care about? You know so much about your customers already, especially if you've followed my advice with the hopes and dreams call. If you gather this data at the beginning of the process, you are one step ahead. If you don't, and you had the opportunity to, you dropped the ball.

For argument's sake, let's say either you weren't able to gather this info during the call or you want to reengage with a former customer. How do you get that information? If you refer to the section on building your brand, you should already have the answer. You should be following or have friended your clients on social media, which gives you an unparalleled view into their lives. That's where people go to talk about themselves so use that to engage and deepen your relationships. Look for common ground because when two people care about the same thing, a relationship can organically develop.

Let's say that one of your former customers isn't on social media and you still aren't able to get that information. What do you do then? It's really simple. Call and talk to them. Call them up and ask them how they're doing. Believe it or not, you have permission to call your past customers. I'm giving it to you right now. I mean, they put their entire financial future in your hands when you gave them a 30-year mortgage. A phone call to check in isn't a bridge too far.

Once you learn these details, immediately enter them into your CRM. That allows you to keep track of and search for these details. You can't be expected to remember this for every single client you've ever had. It's impossible. Forget about the sticky note system; you can pull up a report every month in the Hobbies and Interest section to learn all of the important customer-related dates happening that month.

The Ideal Post-Closing Experience

It's time to create a workflow. That should also sound familiar. If it doesn't, flip back to part five. Just as you want to bucket your various leads and come up with a strategic plan for how to convert those leads, you'll want to do the same thing with your previous customers. This should start as soon as you close the loan. The process should be geared toward helping them prepare for the next steps so they can be easily tackled without any problems. This should also be geared toward helping you expand your business.

I've included what I feel is the best model to delight the customer post-close. Take the time to review and make it personal to you. And take the time to put intentionality behind it so you can ensure these are things you do with every single customer after you close a loan. Don't skip this step or relegate the customer to a dull and irrelevant drip campaign. These relationships can lead to referrals and a deeper relationship within the community.

I've chosen four steps and I'll break each one down. These aren't all my ideas and it's not my own personal system; this is what I've gathered from those who do this exceptionally well. Take what you can use from these examples and tactics to create the ultimate post-closing strategy to thank your customers for their business while creating a path forward toward a deeper, more connected relationship.

Post-Closing: 1 to 5 Days

The loan was just funded, but you still have stuff to do. Get creative in how you engage with your customers. You have this window when a lot of cool stuff is happening in their lives. How can you be a key influence there? Not sure where to start?

One great idea that sounds boring on the surface but ends up being super helpful is to give the customer a copy of all their documents. This serves two purposes. It's convenient for the customer because they don't know when they will need to provide documentation. Also, it prevents them from having to call you if they need something. Get out in front of that and give the customer all of their documents as part of the basic services you provide.

Housewarming parties are another great gesture that can serve more than one purpose. They reward the customer, welcome them to the community, get them acquainted with their new neighbors, and stir up potential business. Remember the loan consultant who arranged for a taco truck to park outside their customer's housewarming party? Why not take that a step further and offer everyone in the area a free taco if they fill out a card with their email address? Is a taco worth an email address? Damn right it is. All day long. I'll give you my email address for a taco right now.

You want to make this moment the celebration of all time! Now you have the chance to come in and do something incredible for the customer; trust me when I say that it's so much better when you do something they don't expect. You can find more original gift ideas later in the chapter, but you don't have to get hung up on gifts and you don't have to spend a ton of money. Get creative. This is the fun part of our job! You know your community better than anyone. If your customers are new to the community, what can you share with them that they might like? Local events, restaurants, activities, the list goes on. Try tapping into what you know and what makes you different as a loan consultant.

Post-Closing: 3 to 7 Days

It's during this time frame that I recommend you make what I refer to as the "business development call." Do you have a set call that happens a certain number of days after funding for you customer? If you don't, you're missing a leveraging opportunity; you've just closed a loan and now it's time for you to go and ask for business referrals. You constantly need to keep your eyes and ears open. I know that's awkward for some people but it's just what we do. If you can't ask for business, you might be in the wrong industry.

Go back to earlier in the process when you requested testimonials. Were you able to get one? If not, or you didn't ask at all, now is the time. Be proactive and hunt down those testimonials and reviews, because every single one you get on a public platform gives you a little more leverage and value in the eyes of a potential new customer. Don't be afraid to ask your customer to share their testimonial on their personal Facebook page and to tag you because that will mean a lot to your business. Yes, dang right you should ask that question because, after this process, you deserve it.

Post-Closing: 30-Plus Days

Even a month after closing, potential issues could still arise. Have you ever had an issue where your customer had a hard time making that first payment, got confused, and then called you to yell at you? You're who they call when they want to yell. I know because it's happened to me plenty of times.

We can all be more responsible for our customers' first payment experience. This is a big one. Get educated, get involved, and lead your customer through this process, so you can answer their questions and provide guidance.

Here's another big thing to consider: Have you ever told your customer that you might sell their loan? It can be confusing for a customer when they suddenly get a goodbye letter and they're being told they need to send their payment elsewhere. The term "goodbye letter" has such a negative connotation, they will naturally be confused if they don't understand the process or what's happening. "We just closed a loan. What do you mean, 'goodbye?'"

You can ease their minds because you can control the customer experience. Going back to the idea of making videos, payments and goodbye letters are two more topics that you can make videos about and work them into your post-closing workflow. Then customers have this information and don't need to call you when they're upset after something unexpected has happened.

Post-Closing: Keep in Touch Monthly

You did their loan, threw them a party, posted a badass review, got a referral, and made sure their first payment is okay. Great! Now how do you maintain this relationship for the rest of your life?

For starters, there are two events in particular when you'll want to reach out to your past customers:

1. **Birthdays:** We all care about our birthdays. Think of how many people on social media wish you a happy birthday. All of those people blend together so you want to do something different to stand out. There's a big difference between sending a happy birthday message on a person's birthday and on the night before, saying something like, "I want to be the first to wish you a happy birthday." Those are two entirely different experiences and it only requires a small tweak. The same is true about wedding anniversaries.

2. **Move-in Days:** As a mortgage professional, you may remember the anniversary of the loan but I guarantee you that your customer doesn't care. What your customer does care about is the day they moved into their home and had pizza on the floor because they didn't have any furniture yet. That's what they remember. Congratulate them on that and become a part of those important life moments.

"That's great, Alec, but what about the other 363 days of the year?" You want to be proactive. You want to do more.

You know how I keep saying that everything is connected. Think back to some of the ways I suggested you attract new customers and forge relationships with real estate agents and utilize some of those techniques. If you're still having trouble getting started, here are some more ideas:

- **Drip campaigns:** I know I've bad-mouthed drip campaigns, but if you are not willing to be intentional and put together a strategy to build a relationship for life, just put your customer on the dreaded drip campaign. It's better than doing nothing and if you are literally doing nothing, that's not acceptable.

- **Community events:** I know a team that hosts a "Think and Drink" at a local restaurant every Thursday. A couple of people on the team go out into the community, have some food, and connect with some human beings in the area to preach the word. Post it on social media. Invite your former customers.

- **Mailers:** This may sound boring and stale but it doesn't have to be. I'm not talking about sending a postcard. What if, instead, you speak to the owner of the restaurant where you go all the time (your third place maybe), and you get some coupons you can send out to your former customers with a note saying, "I was at this restaurant. We had a great time and I think you'll love it too. Here's a gift from the owner." That is so much better than getting a generic postcard that will most likely get lost in the pile of other postcards from your competitors. Stand out. Be different. Be visible.

- **Personal life updates:** It sounds weird but my customers changed my life. Yours probably did too. They are the reason you can support your kids and buy your car. They are your livelihood and the people responsible for providing you the life you want to live. At least, that's the way I look at it, so I like to share what is going on in my life. Relationships are a two-way street. One way involves you learning about your customer on a personal level. The other involves them learning about you and knowing what's going on in your life. This makes some mortgage professionals a little uncomfortable, but to me, it's a no-brainer. If you want a relationship with your customers, you have to go all in. I stumbled upon this by mistake years earlier when, every three months, I'd send out a generic mailer about the company, often in a big 8x11 envelope because those get opened. I included a personal newsletter about my life. I would talk about my new puppy, She-Ra, the princess of power (I'm an '80s kid). I talked about getting married, buying a car, and purchasing my first home. I shared everything, and what happened was that it started to matter to my customers. I wasn't just Alec, the mortgage guy; I was Alec, the community guy. I was Alec, the trusted advisor. Lean in. Have you done that? If not, it's a chance to connect, make an impact, and become visible.

- **Pick up the phone:** It's not always complicated. Not everything has to be a gimmick. And when you hear that coming from me, you know there is some truth to it because I never pass up an opportunity to capitalize on a good gimmick. Sometimes simple is better, and nothing is simpler than picking up the phone and calling your customers. Ask how they're doing. They will ask you about rates if they care about rates, but touch base to make sure they have everything they need.

- **Tax time:** It comes around every single year and homeowners have one document they need—the closing document. The customer has seen and signed so many documents they might not be able to tell which is which or even know where they can find their CD. You could pull the CD and proactively send them out to the customers who purchased a home that year with a note that says something like, "It's tax time, and you're going to need this document." Your customers definitely care about their taxes. This is a really thoughtful way to stay in a relationship.

- **Gift card:** When you know that a customer's kid is going to have a birthday, send them a five-dollar gift card to a yogurt place the day before with a message that says something like, "Take your kid out for a great birthday on me." Heck, make it two dollars. The money doesn't matter. The point is to do something that shows the customer you are thinking about them.

- **Uber coupons:** You can easily send one of these to someone electronically. You can say something like, "Happy Anniversary! Have some adult beverages on the town and use this so you don't have to worry about getting home." It's thoughtful, cute, and most importantly, it gets you out of that predictable box.

Here's your job: Orchestrate a post-closing strategy that works for you. You have to be excited about it. If that's sharing a cool winery with people, be excited. If it's restaurants, community engagement, and charity events, be all in. Why is that important? Well, how often do you do things that you don't like? Probably not that often, so if you don't get excited, it will be more difficult (if not impossible) to make it part of your regular routine.

Not Just Any Gift Will Do

Many consultants send closing gifts, but unfortunately, most don't put much thought into what they send. You can't just send anything. You don't want to send your customer a Starbucks gift card if they hate Starbucks. It's not just what you send, it's the sentiment behind it. A bottle of wine is a bottle of wine—I can get that when checking into a hotel. That doesn't mean that much, but if you send the customer a bottle of wine from your favorite winery in Napa where you know the owner, that gift means something more. If you give them a chance to meet the owner and tour the facility if they are there, that will mean even more.

There is a story that Gary Vee told on a podcast.[15] For those of you who don't know, he sells wine. He was talking about how he sent a customer an autographed jersey of their favorite sports player. It cost him $300 and the guy didn't respond at all. Gary said, "What the heck? That cost me more than I made on the sale of the wine."

Two weeks later, Gary received an order for $5,000 worth of wine, and the person who made the purchase had

---

15 Gary Vee, "The Jay Cutler Story," *YouTube*, July 13, 2016, https://www.youtube.com/watch?v=YwY1gO13VsQ.

gotten his name from the guy Gary bought the jersey for. It's safe to say the referral was much more satisfying than a mere "thank you."

The moral of this story is to know your customers. If you've done your job, you've asked the right questions, so you know what your customers like. If you're going to send a closing gift, use that information. Don't send the crappy bottle of wine. Instead, do something amazing for that customer to bring your relationship to a whole new level.

It may cost a little more to send a thoughtful and memorable gift but try thinking of it another way. You spend money on business development already and relationship building is another form of business development. If you can effectively maintain quality relationships with your previous clients, it could become your number one source of new business.

Go Forth and Build Influence

I started compiling all of the tips, tricks, strategies, lessons, and theories to put into this book over two years ago, but I never expected to learn as much as I did on this journey. Along the way, I have become more convinced than ever that the single-most important characteristic that will define the success of future mortgage professionals will be their ability to develop influence in their communities and online.

You've just read the book. I don't need to tell you that local mortgage professionals (and really all local, referral-based sales professionals) are being bypassed because the consumer is operating differently during the home financing process. We're becoming invisible because the traditional methods of standing behind referral partners has slowly deteriorated as the world becomes more digital and comes online.

Think back to the credit crisis. The world of mortgage lending as we knew it ended. Companies shut down every day. Professionals had to redefine themselves and radically change their business and their strategies because they couldn't keep doing what they were doing before. Those who couldn't make that change were left behind but those who survived were able to adapt. The same thing is happening now. It may be happening at a much slower pace but don't assume that you can keep doing the same thing. I see too many mortgage professionals who refuse to change. Instead, they get frustrated or double down on old strategies. They hold on to techniques that aren't nearly as relevant anymore. Some are able to get by to a certain degree, but it's harder because their years of experience are being marginalized and commoditized as time progresses.

The good news is we don't have to go extinct. We don't have to be invisible. It starts by stepping out from behind your desk, leaving the office, and getting out with the people in your community to serve, educate, and engage with them face-to-face. It also means going online to develop a powerful personal brand that showcases to the world what you stand for, what you believe in, what your business is about, the level of service you provide, and what customers can expect. It requires posting, marketing, and most importantly, campaigning in order to create influence. And if you take only one lesson from this book let it be this—embrace the power of video. Video is the most powerful tool you have at your disposal to create influence. Turn around the camera, hit the record button, and put yourself out into the world. Become visible, get yourself online, and earn your place in the spotlight so you can build your influence!

For many of you, making this pivot and changing with the times requires learning a brand-new skill set. I'm not going to sugarcoat it or lie to you and say that it will be easy because it won't be for everyone. Becoming visible once again doesn't happen on its own. The trick to everything we've covered in this book is to make all of this second nature, and that will take some time. You want to become hardwired to search for and engage with your clients on social media. You want to get in the habit of gathering information from conversations and social media feeds and putting it into your CRM so you can follow up and use it later. You want to get to the point where you don't even think about that stuff. You want to constantly build a rapport with customers and strengthen your relationships. You want to get used to posting articles and filming videos. It should be part of your routine.

None of this happens on its own or organically. When you first start out, you need to be intentional and strategic because there will be a learning curve and there will be growing pains. You will not be good at everything. You will not succeed every time out. Your first couple of videos and articles might be terrible, but don't let that deter you. Stick to the plan because that will allow you to be consistent. You can't just do it some of the time. You have to do it every time. When you start out, it's the consistency that is the most important thing.

You might be excited now to make a drastic change but we are all human and we can't stay excited forever. Trust me, I've tried. Your enthusiasm will wane, no matter how good your intentions or your ideas. Change is hard. Stepping outside of your comfort zone is hard, so try to think of ways to hold yourself accountable. Everyone is different, and you know yourself and your tendencies much better than I do. Maybe for you, an accountability partner will help keep you on track. That person could be a coworker or a manager. Ask for their help. Heck, do it together! Create a competition inside your office with your colleagues if you have to. I constantly look for ways to motivate myself and recently created a challenge to post 100 videos in 100 days. Whatever works and fuels you to keep going is worth trying.

If you feel yourself slowly becoming irrelevant, you can make that change to become visible once again; at the end of the day, it's on you. You are the only one responsible for making that change. I am a massive believer that you have to just go out and do it. Life isn't in the waiting process, the learning process, or the overthinking process—it's in the action process. It doesn't matter if it's a podcast, a video series, or the next piece of content—do it. You will get over the awkwardness, just like you got over the awkwardness associated with cold calls and going to open houses years earlier. You will make mistakes and you will screw up, but that's how you learn and improve. Go out there and do it, because if you continue to sit and wait for the perfect time, you will never be part of the action. Whatever you've been resistant to or holding back on starting, don't wait any longer. Go all in. It will change your life!

ACKNOWLEDGEMENTS

When I started on my journey to understand the changing dynamics reshaping the job of the modern mortgage professional, I never imagined where it would take me. There are a ton of people around me professionally today who contributed to this work simply by being awesome and leading from the front. That's really the amazing thing about social media and the internet as it exists today. If you just listen and have an eagerness to learn, all the information is available to you. But, there are also a lot of people who played significant roles in my professional development at one point or another. Some for longer periods of time, and some for just moments. But those moments with all these people taught me valuable lessons I'll never forget. And for that, I'm so humbly thankful. I thought about listing out all the teachings and lessons I've learned from the people below, but that seems impossible. I was told once that I was just an extra in the movie of the lives of the people around me. If that's the case, then you all below played one hell of a role in the movie of my professional life so far and the impact was incredible. Thank you to Dan Hanson, Anthony Hsieh, John Bianchi, Kevin Budde, David Kravitz, Jay Kunkle, Brigitte Ataya, Kevin Reskey, Tammy Richards,

Dean Bloxom, Jay Johnson, Angelo Mozilo, Brian Hale, Tom Hunt, Greg Sayegh, Dave Bochsler, Diana Macfarlane, Brian Decker, Josh Pitts, Scott Groves, Brian Covey, Dave Savage, Todd Duncan, Barry Habib, David Norris, and Gary Vaynerchuk.

CPSIA information can be obtained
at www.ICGtesting.com
Printed in the USA
FSHW012324170821
84037FS

9 781734 578300